CLEANING SUPERVISOR'S HANDBOOK

CLEANING SUPERVISOR'S HANDBOOK

J. K. P. EDWARDS
T.D., M.A., M.I.Mgt., F.B.I.C.Sc.

Formerly
Technical director

Russell Kirby Limited

CRESTA PUBLISHING

PUBLISHED BY:

THE CRESTA PUBLISHING COMPANY,
14 Beechfield Road,
Liverpool L18 3EH
Tel: 0151 722 7400

PRODUCED BY:

GARNETT DICKINSON PUBLISHING,
Eastwood Works,
Fitzwilliam Road,
Rotherham S65 1JU
Tel: 01709 364721

First published in 1984
Second impression in 1985
Third impression in 1987
Second edition 1991
Third edition 1992
Fourth edition 2001

© J. K. P. Edwards, 1984

ISBN 0 947567 45 3

PREFACE

"SUPERVISORS are a fortunate lot for, as everyone knows, they stroll around with nothing to do – except –

Decide what is to be done, ask somebody to do it, listen to reasons why it should not be done, or why it should be done by somebody else, or why it should be done in this way and then prepare arguments in rebuttall that are convincing and conclusive.

Follow up to see if the job has been done, discover that it has not been done, enquire why it has not been done, listen to excuses from the person who did not do it and then think up arguments to overcome the excuses.

Follow up a second time to see if the job has been done, discover that it has been done incorrectly, point out how it should be done, conclude that as long as it has been done it might as well be left as it is, wonder if it were not the time to get rid of the person who cannot do the job correctly and reflect that in all probability any successor would be just as bad or worse.

Consider how much more simply and better the job would have been done had the supervisor done it himself in the first place. Reflect satisfactorily that if the job had been done by himself he would have been able to do it right in 20 minutes and that, as things turned out, he had spent 2 days to find out why it was that it had taken somebody else 3 weeks to do it wrong. And employers imagine that a supervisor HAS NOTHING TO DO".

It can truly be said that GOOD CLEANING SUPERVISORS ARE WORTH THEIR WEIGHT IN GOLD.

It is recognised that perhaps the vast majority of cleaning supervisors are women. In order to simplify the text, however, the word 'he', rather than 'he-she', has been used throughout as the latter is somewhat cumbersome and would have hindered the natural flow of the text.

ACKNOWLEDGEMENTS

I am very grateful to my wife, Madeleine, for her constructive and helpful advice and to Miss Eleanor Smears for the illustrations. I thank St. John Ambulance for their help with the section on First Aid and Coy's of St. Helens Limited for their permission to reproduce the section on Commercial Phrases.

CONTENTS

1

PRINCIPLES OF CLEANING

Definitions

Clean is defined as "free from dirt" and dirt is defined as "matter in the wrong place." Cleaning is, therefore, the removal of dirt but how clean is clean? The answer to this question will vary depending upon circumstances. For example a hospital operating theatre could only be described as clean if it is spotless and free from harmful bacteria. An office might be described as clean if there are no visible signs of dirt and litter. The floor of an engineering factory may be considered clean if there are no bits of swarf or metal tubing visible on the floor even though oil and grease may be present but at an acceptable level. Whatever the building, or location within a building, the need exists for efficient maintenance of the working environment. Cleaning is motivated by both economic and aesthetic considerations and our present civilisation is characterised by certain standards of cleanliness and hygiene which it is our responsibility to maintain.

Advantages of a clean and hygienic environment

Some advantages of working in a clean and hygienic environment are:
Improved morale.
Improved health.
A visible sign that employers care for their employees.
Improved productivity.
Reduced absenteeism.
Pride by employees in their place of work.
Disincentive to abuse the building by vandalism and graffiti.
A visible sign of efficiency thereby promoting good relations between management and staff.
Minimises the risk of accidents.
Occupants are more likely to keep their place of work in a clean and tidy condition.

Cleaning standards

It has already been mentioned that cleaning standards will vary depending upon the location. One of the first tasks facing a supervisor responsible for cleaning a particular area is to ascertain the standard of cleanliness required. A supervisor should be aware of the difficulties that are involved in setting cleaning standards as part of a general awareness of the overall cleaning

1

problems associated with a particular location. The main factors that should be taken into account when setting the standard of cleanliness for an area are:

Who is to set the standard? e.g. In a hospital would it be the pathologist, ward sister or domestic manager?

To what use is the area put? e.g. An operating theatre or a bin yard.

Who is to inspect the area on a regular basis?

What is the standard of cleanliness required e.g. high, medium or basic?

Does 'clean' mean 'free from visible dirt' or 'free from harmful bacteria'?

How often can the area be cleaned?

Is there sufficient money available to achieve the standards required?

Who is to authorise the expenditure?

Is the time allowed for cleaning adequate?

Are the staff available?

Are the staff trained to the required standard?

Are there any obstructions that should be removed?

Does the nature of the surfaces to be cleaned present a problem?

What are the types of dirt expected?

The first step is to decide the standard for each particular area in a building. This is normally carried out by means of a survey which entails visiting each part of the premises, deciding the standard required and writing a cleaning specification for each area. The cleaning specification will include the method of working, materials and equipment required and any particular problems that are liable to be encountered as for example anti-static surfaces in operating theatres. The next step is to train staff and demonstrate the standards required in all areas and to ensure that these standards are achieved. Subsequently each area should be checked periodically to ensure that the required standard is being maintained. It is strongly recommended that a check list is designed for use in prestige and vital areas to ensure that all the really important aspects are covered and not overlooked.

The cleaning specification will include details regarding the frequency of cleaning and whether an area is to be treated daily, weekly or periodically. Details regarding frequency are particularly important in cleaning specifications for schools where much of the heavy work, including stripping of old polish from floors, re-sealing and high level dusting, normally is carried out during school holiday periods.

Preventive maintenance

It is convenient to include in this section some notes on preventive maintenance. This means a continuous maintenance programme with the aim of preventing break-down of machinery and equipment and maintaining them in continuous working order. Whilst much has been talked about preventive maintenance very little generally is carried out. The normal practice is to use a machine or piece of equipment until eventually it stops functioning and then urgent action is required to mend it. This can be expensive particularly if maintenance engineers need to make unscheduled visits.

Preventive maintenance is achieved by devising a maintenance schedule for each piece of machinery and equipment and then ensuring that the item concerned is maintained in the correct manner on the due date. A simple visual chart is probably the best means of maintaining a record. A chart serves as a permanent reminder to a supervisor that equipment should be maintained on a regular basis.

Some of the benefits that can be gained by effective preventive maintenance are:

Minimum breakdown of machinery.
Most effective use of machinery.
Most effective use of labour.
Minimum expenditure in repair costs saves money.
Greatly reduced risk of accidents due to faulty machinery.
Longer working life of machinery and equipment.

ORGANISATION AND SUPERVISION

Definition of a supervisor

A supervisor, in broad terms, may be defined as a person who is responsible for:

The conduct of others in the achievement of a particular task or tasks.
The maintenance of standards.
The issue, use and care of materials and equipment under his control.
Services to be rendered by the workers under his control.

Cleaners are responsible for carrying out tasks allotted to them. The supervisor is primarily responsible for making things happen through the efforts of other people. He is responsible for people, materials, equipment and productivity.

The word 'supervisor' can, in one organisation, refer to the senior working cleaner. In another organisation it may refer to an executive who works at planning level and is, in fact, a top management executive.

For our purposes, however, we shall define a supervisor as the person in direct overall charge of a team of cleaners who is responsible for all aspects of work. Basically he has three functions those of foreman, instructor and representative.

As a foreman he is responsible for planning and directing the activities of his cleaners towards the objectives set for his group.

As an instructor he must assure himself that his cleaners are properly trained to carry out the instructions given to them. In practice he often has to carry out the training himself.

As a representative he has a dual responsibility: simultaneously he must represent his staff to management and management to his staff.

Five requirements of a supervisor

Although a supervisor must be a person of many talents perhaps these requirements are the most important:

Knowledge of the technical aspects of the job. This means a knowledge of machines, materials, products and processes which is obtained from on-the-job experience, apprenticeship and/or special training courses.
Knowledge of his duties and responsibilities. This involves a knowledge of the functions of management and the organisational structure and policy of the company and an ability to analyse and classify his own duties.
Skill in instruction. This demands a knowledge of all phases of the procedures undertaken by his staff and the ability to communicate his knowledge effectively. He must have a systematic approach to instruction and skill in communicating knowledge to his cleaners.
Skill in improving methods. He must be able to recognise problems relating to staff, machines, materials and methods and devise solutions.
Skill in leading. He must have the knack of winning the co-operation of his

group of cleaners, an understanding of the relationship between people and the qualities of tact, patience and fair mindedness.

Basic supervisory tasks

Planning: is the process of setting out the objectives of the group, anticipating the conditions which will have to be met and determining future courses of action in line with the objectives and with changing conditions. The supervisor must plan the work of the group and of individual cleaners in an orderly manner with due regard for the relationship of one worker to another to produce minimum friction and maximum productivity.

Organising: is the installation of efficient work methods and routines to obtain maximum results from cleaners, materials and equipment with minimum expenditure of money.

Executing: is seeing that the plans he has made and the methods he has initiated are carried out, and continue to be carried out, with the desired result.

Evaluating and Improving: are assessing the effectiveness of his plans and methods, diagnosing weaknesses in them and being alert for means of refining and improving them.

Duties and responsibilities of a supervisor

These may vary in detail according to the size and structure of an organisation but basically a supervisor is responsible for:

Induction training of new cleaners and training experienced cleaners in new methods.

Communications both within his group and between his group and others.

Safety in the working environment and the physical welfare of his cleaners.

Efficient production in accordance with the objectives of the organisation.

Personal qualities of a supervisor

A supervisor must possess many desirable qualities of which perhaps the most important are:

Efficiency: is good personal organisation and a "head for detail". If the supervisor cannot function efficiently he will not set a good example for his staff or inspire confidence in himself.

Diplomacy: is skill in dealing with people. He must be "the boss" without being "bossy", firm but fair and be able to keep discipline without arousing resentment.

Integrity: is being honest and conscientious in his dealings with both staff and management.

Reliability: is being a stable character. He must be the kind of man who willingly accepts responsibility and cares about the quality of his work.

5

Organisation

The capability and efficiency of any organisation depends on its being formulated initially to specifications which are most suited to the objectives to be achieved. Organisational structures need to be examined from time to time and reviewed to bring them up to date. Organisation should be based firstly on the work to be done and secondly on the people available. The job takes preference over personalities.

The job of a supervisor is onerous. It requires not only knowledge of how the work should be done but also the ability to assess the situation objectively.

Link between management and cleaners

A supervisor is in direct contact with cleaners and is the link between management and the cleaning staff. A supervisor should:

Know management policy with regard to cleaning the area under his control.

Be clearly aware of the limits of his authority and responsibility.

Know intimately the area for which he is responsible.

Be able to convey information both up to management and down to the cleaning staff.

Be able to advise both management and cleaners with a foot in both camps.

Be aware of the resources in manpower and financial assistance on which he can call in the event of an emergency.

Be loyal to both management and cleaning staff.

Have leadership qualities.

Promote a team spirit.

Set a good example at all times.

Know his cleaners' capabilities and personal problems.

Have a sense of fair play.

Create the right environment at work both to motivate cleaners and minimise absenteeism.

Enforce safety regulations.

Be able to train new staff.

Have the welfare of his staff in mind.

Line management

A supervisor is a member of 'line management' by which is meant that one supervisor is in charge of a group of people. All orders and reports should be passed up or down a single 'line' and each person should be responsible to only one superior. Each cleaner should be responsible to only one supervisor and, in turn, each supervisor should be responbsible to only one manager. If a cleaner is responsible to two supervisors he would have great difficulty in serving both well and would inevitably favour one at the expense of the other. It is, therefore, important that the authority and responsibility of each supervisor in an organisation is clearly defined so that everyone knows for what he is responsible and decisions can be made at the correct level. Clear definition also ensures that the duties and responsibilities of two people do not overlap thus preventing the inevitable friction that could occur under such circumstances.

Job description

To overcome problems of overlap each supervisor should be issued with a job description in which his authority and responsibility are clearly defined together with any limitation as for example whether a supervisor may, or may not, authorise overtime.

Responsibilities of a supervisor to employer and employees

A supervisor has a responsibility both towards his employer and to his cleaning staff. The main responsibilities of a supervisor towards his employer are to:

Ensure company policy is carried out at all times.
Ensure cleaning staff work to maximum efficiency.
Obtain the required cleaning output at minimum cost.
Maintain discipline among the cleaning staff.
Minimise waste of labour and materials.
Advise his superior as to what is actually happening and to pass up both suggestions and grievances.
Pass orders from above to his cleaning staff.
Explain to his cleaning staff any changes in policy or operation which may be decreed by management.
Ensure his staff are trained efficiently.
Reduce absenteeism to a minimum.
Report any particular shortcomings amongst his staff.
Ensure compliance with any regulations which may be in force.

A supervisor also has a responsibility towards his cleaners. Some of his main responsibilities are to:

Have concern for their health, safety, welfare and morale.
Train cleaners to the required standard.
Ensure that each cleaner understands the job for which he is responsible.
Create a good working atmosphere for his cleaners.
Give simple clear instructions.
Be impartial and have no favourites.
Allocate easy and hard jobs on a rota system.
Ensure that all cleaners comply with any regulations as for example the Factories Act.

Supervisor's responsibility for Health and Safety

A supervisor should be concerned with both the mental and physical aspects of his cleaners health and welfare. Examples are:
Mental

7

Settling grievances by discussion or by passing information to the supervisor's manager.

Sorting out problems both those relating to work and to a lesser extent domestic.

Training cleaners to the required degree of skill and safety.

Physical

Ensuring the provision of clean overalls and protective clothing.

Ensuring cleaners receive a clothing allowance where applicable.

Sorting pay problems.

Arranging adequate tea breaks.

Allocating locker space.

Arranging for a rest room to be provided and ensuring that it is adequately maintained.

Arranging a holiday rota.

Arranging transport on public holidays.

Ensuring staff receive travel allowance where appropriate.

Ensuring heating, lighting and ventilation are adequate.

Advising on personal hygiene problems if required.

Being aware of first-aid procedures in the event of sickness or accident.

Ensuring staff have cafeteria facilities if appropriate.

Work schedules

One of the tasks frequently given to a supervisor is that of preparing work schedules for his cleaners. A work schedule ensures that each cleaner knows exactly what he has to do and when it should be done. This is an important part of a supervisor's job and preparation of a work schedule should be given due consideration.

Factors that should be taken into account when planning a work schedule are as follows:

Time necessary to complete each job.

A time allowance for meal breaks.

How many staff are required and how many are available.

The location of the area.

The exact area to be cleaned.

The equipment required.

An allocation of jobs to each person.

The standard of cleanliness required for each area.

The time at which cleaning can be carried out.

The cash available for the job.

Type of furniture and fittings in the area to be cleaned.

Any particular requirements of the customer or owner of the premises.

That all tasks are carried out in a logical sequence.

Availability of equipment.

Any special equipment or materials needed.

Duty rota

It is normally a supervisor's job to plan duty rotas for cleaning staff. Factors that should be considered when planning a duty rota are as follows:

Type of area concerned.

Number of hours required to clean the area.

Frequency of cleaning.

Ensuring all areas are covered.

Particular coverage for priority areas.

Number of staff needed for the job.

Number of staff available.

Whether shifts or split duties are needed.

Whether week-end and evening work is to be included.

Attempt to avoid late working on one day with an early start next day.

Number of relief staff available.

Cover for sickness.

Cover for absence and rest days.

Arrangements for rest days and days off.

Knowledge of which staff prefer certain days off.

Cover for holidays and bank holidays.

Arrangements in the event of compassionate leave being necessary.

Off duty days for friends to be together if possible.

Friends to work same shift all week.

Whether an allowance should be made for overtime.

Any financial limitations.

Whether any particular time is unsuitable, or unavailable, for cleaning any specific area.

Whether staff can read English or whether a visual diagram would be preferable.

Arrangements should be fair to all.

Rotas should not break any regulations e.g. working agreements.

It is recommended that a duty rota should be in the form of a chart which is sufficiently large to be easily read. It should be marked using different colours with each cleaner's days off, rest days and holidays shown clearly. Departmental areas, names of cleaners, dates and week-ends should be in capital letters to avoid confusion. A duty rota should be posted on a notice board at least two days, but preferably a week, in advance or longer if possible. Alterations inevitably will be necessary from time to time and these should be indicated clearly.

Night shifts

From time to time it may be necessary to arrange a night shift for cleaning staff. If a night shift becomes necessary the following factors should be considered to ensure that the night shift functions smoothly and efficiently

The aim of the night shift should be clearly defined in cleaning terms.

The hours to be worked should be stated.

9

The standard required should be fully discussed with the person in charge of the night shift.

A method of work should be agreed.

Machines, equipment and materials should be checked.

One person should be designated to take charge of the night shift.

Special feeding arrangements may be necessary.

Break times should be clearly defined.

Toilet facilities should be available.

Special transport should be arranged if necessary.

Any special pay allowance should be discussed and agreed prior to starting.

The supervisor in charge of the night shift should be given the telephone number of a person to contact in case of difficulty.

Security of the premises during the night should be agreed with the occupier of the building.

Managing time

Napoleon is reported to have said to his Generals "Gentlemen I can give you anything but time". Most supervisors constantly work against time. Almost all supervisors are hard pressed with too many tasks and too little time in which to complete them. A supervisor is often heard to say "I want to do this and that but I just don't have the time".

Most supervisors would agree that there are not enough working hours in the day. Most would also agree that a great many working hours are wasted – and there does not seem to be much that can be done about it. Whilst there is no magic formula to automatically give anyone more hours in the day an indication of how time is wasted, if it is unplanned, can be helpful.

Some actions which indicate a failure to manage time effectively are:

Snap decisions.

Over-ruling subordinates.

Over attention to detail.

Personal favours for "old customers" which disrupt schedules.

Other involvement of subordinates in decisions not affecting them.

Postponement of meetings (wasting subordinates time).

Unnecessary overtime for certain cleaners because he is too busy to meet them.

Over active in outside activities.

Encouraging interruptions by his colleagues.

Changing the agenda of a training session or other meeting without consideration.

Carrying out minor tasks himself – failure to delegate.

Typical results from this type of behaviour are:

Ineffective decisions.

Supervisor complains "no-one keeps me informed of the extent of problems around here".

Personal attacks on subordinates.

Tension on the part of both supervisors and cleaners resulting in:

Personal health problems.

Back-biting and lack of team work.

Lack of job satisfaction for both supervisor and cleaners.

To manage time effectively it is recommended that a supervisor should:

Keep a detailed written time log over a period of perhaps one week and study it to find out how the time has been spent.

Ask himself "what are the things that take time and contribute nothing? What would happen if they weren't done at all? Am I giving the right amount of time to the really important things?" Learn to say "No".

Allocate solid blocks of uninterrupted time for the things that really matter – the important decisions that have to be made.

Devise simple systems to deal with frequently recurring jobs to enable more jobs to be delegated.

Use check lists for example inspection schedules.

Use a "year to view" wall chart.

Draw up a schedule of pending jobs – sort out priorities.

Plan big jobs thoroughly well in advance.

Make written notes of any important decisions so that the same topics will not be discussed over and over again.

Before training staff or carrying out an important cleaning operation ensure all equipment is working and ready for use.

Delegation

The dictionary definition of delegation is "entrusting of authority to a deputy". However hard working a supervisor may be it is not his job to carry the total work of any department. Indeed if he did so he would be failing in his task which is to organise the work within his department so that it can be carried out by others. A supervisor's job is to ensure that results are achieved according to the overall management plan. Whilst it is essential that a supervisor knows how to do his subordinate's jobs, preferably being able to do them as well as or better than the cleaners themselves, he must be seen to be in control of the whole department and not totally involved in any particular part of it.

Many supervisors take the easy way out. They tell themselves that it would take far longer to explain to someone else how a job should be done than to do it themselves. Whilst this is probably true if the situation continues to repeat itself it becomes apparent that the supervisor is not effective. Time taken to describe to a subordinate how a repetitive job should be done will clearly produce results over a period of time. A supervisor's time is more valuable to an organisation than a cleaner's time and this fact should always be born in mind.

As a job expands supervisors are sometimes found working with the cleaners to cope with the additional work involved. Whilst this may be necessary in the short term if the situation persists the supervisors should try to persuade management that another cleaner is required, if only on a part-time basis, to cope with additional work and thereby allow the supervisor to function effectively. Supervisors are not paid to be cleaners and they must accept this fact.

It is often difficult for a supervisor to recognise when to delegate. Some supervisors tend to cling to almost every duty themselves thereby giving the impression that no-one else is capable of doing that particular job. It is in their own interests to ensure that as many jobs as possible are delegated so that they can carry out their main task which is that of supervision.

Some of the signs that should indicate to a supervisor that more delegation is necessary are, firstly, being approached by operatives to make a decision on even the most trivial matters. Secondly finding oneself doing a job that could quite easily be done by a subordinate. Thirdly finding one has not time to plan activities, look ahead or effect proper supervision over those under his control. Lack of time often shows itself by supervisors working excessive hours in order to cope with the job. This state of affairs is far more common than is generally realised and often leads to domestic problems resulting in domestic upheaval. Fourthly constant interruptions by subordinates asking for a decision, instructions, guidance and advice can be very time consuming and interrupt any train of thought a supervisor may be engaged in at that particular time.

Any or all of the above indicate that more delegation is not just desirable but essential.

It is important to recognise that when considering delegation of jobs to subordinates one is only considering transfer of authority to them and not the responsibility. The responsibility must remain with the supervisor. He is totally responsible for all the activities of his department. The authority to do a particular task can be delegated to a subordinate but the responsibility of ensuring that the job is correctly carried out must remain with the supervisor. It is, therefore, imperative that the person to whom the job is delegated is aware of exactly what is required of him so that he can effectively carry out the task. When delegating a job, therefore, it is important to spend as much time as possible explaining the full implications of the job to ensure that the person concerned understands exactly what is required.

How to delegate

Perhaps the best approach is for a supervisor to write down each job he is doing. These tasks should be listed one underneath the other including not only the important essential parts of the job but also the less important periodic tasks. Against each task note those that should be carried out only by the supervisor. Also note those that could be carried out by some other person either now or after training. When considering which jobs can be delegated to others it is important not to delegate a job that is far beyond the capabilities of the person in mind. It is also important not to over delegate to such an extent that the cleaners become over loaded and unable to cope. In this event they will merely become resentful and probably will leave. On the other hand some delegation of the more important jobs gives those concerned a feeling of job satisfaction and job fulfilment and helps to make them feel an important part of the team.

12

Start by giving out those jobs which can be delegated easily. Choose the person concerned and explain fully what is involved and allow him to get on with it. It is important when explaining any task to a person that he is given discretion to make his own decisions should certain circumstances arise which have not been foreseen. It is appreciated that not every decision taken by the person concerned will be correct. In this event the supervisor must ask himself whether he has given all the facts to the person to enable him to make the correct decision. It may well be that some important factor was withheld so that the decision was made in the light of only part of the total facts. If a decision turns out to be wrong the situation should be discussed with the person concerned so that he can understand the error in his method. A supervisor sometimes makes the mistake of jumping to conclusions and admonishing the person concerned in front of others. This will only make the cleaner resentful and he will quickly revert to referring any minor decision to his supervisor.

It has been said earlier that in delegation a supervisor is delegating authority and not responsibility. If, therefore, a subordinate makes a mistake the supervisor must accept responsibility. Every supervisor is responsible for the action of his subordinates whether right or wrong. This is part of the the job for which a supervisor is paid and he must accept the responsibility with the job. If an error is made try and let the person concerned correct the error himself preferably before any harm is done. If, however, the job turns out right then the subordinate will be only too happy to accept the praise that should go with it.

If any training is required before delegation ensure that the person concerned has received all the necessary training either from the supervisor or from some other outside agency. No cleaner can be expected to carry out a job efficiently if he has not been trained.

Work should be delegated gradually so that a person is not overloaded. Many cleaners are middle aged or elderly people and learning new methods and techniques may take longer than would be the case with younger people. It will be necessary for the supervisor to be patient and to persevere if the desired results are to be obtained. However the effort will be worthwhile and the minutes spent in delegating will reap hours in reward.

To summarise how jobs should be delegated to subordinates:

Consider when to delegate.

Write down all jobs and list the names of those cleaners who could do them if they were trained.

Select first simple jobs for delegation.

Explain to the selected person exactly what the job is and make that person's authority absolutely clear.

Do not delegate to separate people jobs which overlap.

Arrange training if necessary.

Delegate the thinking and decision making as well as the doing.

Delegate slowly and gradually.

Do not be over protective and do not check up constantly on his work.

However watch carefully from a distance during early stages and set up a fail safe system to minimise any possible damage as for example alert other supervisors as to what may happen in one's absence.

Stand by his decisions and accept responsibility for them.

If a wrong decision is made do not admonish a cleaner as nothing destroys confidence faster. Just suggest other solutions as being worth a thought next time.

If a criticism cannot be avoided never do it in public. Suggest alternatives only in private.

Remember most decisions have a 50:50 chance of being right and it must have made sense to him at the time. Be patient – and persevere..

Efficiency

Modern society has expanded both qualitatively and quantitatively at a very fast pace. Where once efficiency was desirable it is now necessary for survival. The very rate of growth and change makes it difficult for us to deal with this problem. The old techniques for achieving efficiency simply do not work in the new and ever changing sociological and technological system.

Job design must change because the needs of the cleaners have changed. Some jobs are still broken down into their simplest components but today's higher educated employees demand a meaningful "whole job". Jobs must fit the abilities and aspirations of the people doing them. An employee's attitude is a result of the behaviour which is required of him and motivation results from his sense of achievement.

If jobs do not allow achievement they will be approached mechanically.

Jobs must give the opportunity for rewarding work. Inefficiency is due to the lack of proper utilisation of people and any organisation must be efficient in order to survive. To be efficient the human needs of the cleaners must be met.

The whole purpose of an organisation is to organise men, money and materials into the most efficient production of goods and services and it is the function of supervisors to make sure this happens.

How is efficiency achieved? The answer would appear to be the application of techniques to:

(a) Break the job down into its simplest components with the resultant work performed in a routine mechanistic way.

(b) Motivate the cleaner to produce more by offering more money through piece work or other forms of incentives.

(c) Reduce errors by the use of control procedures and close supervision.

This method works to a degree. However by "amputating talent", by reducing the requirements of every job level to fit the minimum capabilities of people likely to hold those jobs, the chances of error are reduced but it discourages those with higher abilities from doing the most efficient work possible in their task.

Many organisations fail to utilise the full talents of their staff. As a result people do not give of their best. For maximum efficiency, therefore, organisations must take into account the "human needs" of employees at all levels.

14

All members of an organisation are concerned about the future no matter at what level of management a person finds himself. Whilst supervisors may not be in a position to give a final decision on any particular project ideas and support can be given to those who do make these decisions.

Everyday decisions involve risks and the temptation is to put limited resources to solve problems rather than promote opportunities. One leading management consultant indicated that this is an incorrect approach and the correct attitude should be to "starve the problems and feed the opportunities".

The first rule is to discard past projects which have ceased to be productive and to ensure that no more resources, particularly those of manpower, are invested in the no longer productive past. Any manpower available should be transferred and put to work on the opportunities of tomorrow.

A supervisor who wants to be effective should examine periodically all activities and tasks carried out by himself and those he controls from the point of asking "Is this job worth doing?" If it is not the job should be got rid of. The supervisor is then able to concentrate on the few tasks that, if done with excellence, will really make a difference to the results of his own job and the performance of his unit.

A decision is always a choice among options often with another option which is to do nothing. Dissenting opinions often disclose creative solutions which a supervisor has not thought of.

A supervisor's decision is often an instinctive reaction to something that is bothering him. If he tests this reaction against some dissenting opinions he can develop a logical solution rather than an instictive one.

Decisions are often made on the basis of who is right rather than what is right. When a supervisor encourages other views he should make sure the personality of the dissenter does not affect the final decision.

No supervisor is completely without prejudice. His own opinions often reflect his prejudices but because of his position his arguments carry weight. Honest dissent can overcome this.

Many decisions are the right solutions to the wrong problems. Dissent often uncovers the fact that the problem has been defined incorrectly.

An effective decision is often a compromise between strongly opposed points of view. In order to make the best compromise, one which will work in the long term, all sides must be allowed to make their strongest case.

Those who argue for fact, rather than opinions, often forget that the facts can usually be found to support any preconceived opinions.

A good supervisor takes advantage of the experience of his staff and his associates in making his decisions. These people often have opinions backed by their experience and sometimes lack immediate facts to back them up.

By gathering all these 'for' and 'against' opinions the supervisor can decide what facts are needed to make the best choice of options in the final decision.

Whilst it is comforting when everybody is in agreement on a course of action it should be recognised that facts are sometimes not as important as opinions and that dissenting opinions are an essential ingredient of the discussion that leads to good decisions.

When making a decision a supervisor should bear in mind that a decision is not a popularity contest and good decisions are not made by acclamation.

To arrive at an effective decision a supervisor should, therefore, write down all courses of action that should be considered. The strongest possible arguments, both for and against each course, should then be listed in two columns. The correct decision to make should then become apparent. If not the golden rule is 'when in doubt don't'. Allow more time when factors may change tipping the balance in favour of a particular course of action.

Productivity

Productivity is the ratio of input to output. Productivity can be raised by getting more out proportionally than is put in. This will result in cutting the unit cost of production. For example if a cleaner using an ordinary round mop and bucket takes 20 minutes to damp mop an area of 100m^2 and this is later reduced to 10 minutes using a larger bucket on wheels combined with a long stranded mop and a geared wringer then his productivity has been increased.

How a supervisor can improve productivity

Improvement in productivity helps an organisation to become more competitive. Costs are constantly increasing and one of the duties of a supervisor is to ensure that they are minimised. Some of the ways by which a supervisor can influence the productivity of his department are as follows:

Request work study to be carried out leading to work schedules.
Ensure all cleaning staff are cost conscious.
Ensure all staff are trained to the necessary standard.
Ensure, as far as possible, that equipment is up to date and working efficiently.
Use leadership skills to promote a team spirit.
Deal with complaints promptly.
Create a good working atmosphere.
Attempt to motivate cleaners by all means possible.
Involve workers at all levels in an attempt to minimise time lost, absenteeism and labour turnover.
Attempt to ensure all cleaners have an equal share of work.
Do not become overtired.
Make sure that the next job is ready to minimise time lost in preparation.
Control materials to minimise waste.
Stop cleaners carrying out repetitive unnecessary tasks.

A cost conscious supervisor is constantly on the look out to find ways to improve productivity. Some of the ways a supervisor can minimise the waste of time and material by his cleaners are as follows:

"Attempt to ensure that all cleaners have an equal share of work"

Time

Devise simple systems to deal with frequently recurring jobs.
Delegate more tasks to allow greater time for supervision.
Use check lists.
Use wall charts.
Sort out cleaners' priorities.
Prepare a job schedule for each job.
Frequently inspect each area.
Ensure equipment is in constant working order.
Ensure materials are available when required.
Ensure any grievance is dealt with quickly.
Plan big jobs well in advance.
Carry out work study procedures.

Materials

Issue correct amount only.
Train staff in correct method of use.
Check that staff are using materials correctly.
Return any unused materials to store.
Maintain accurate stock records.

Controlling overtime

On occasions overtime will be necessary perhaps to spruce up prestige areas before an important visit. Overtime is, however, often worked unnecessarily resulting in additional costs. Some of the reasons for this are:

Basic wage is too low.
Overtime is offered to attract labour.
Authority for overtime is at too low a level of management.
Bad planning and flow of work.
Poor information given to management.

Management do not know if overtime is necessary.
Restrictive practices.
Poor supervision.
Not enough machinery or equipment.
Poor co-operation with other departments.

In today's economic climate a supervisor should be constantly seeking ways to improve productivity. Those who are successful eventually should reap the reward due.

Control of materials

A supervisor responsible for the use of cleaning materials and equipment should bring his influence to bear on their efficient storage and use. A supervisor can promote efficiency with regard to the control of materials and equipment by:

Having a safe locked store.
Ensuring that the size of store is adequate for both equipment and materials.
Arranging for a sink to be available for cleaning brushes, mops, pads etc.
Arranging for each cleaner to have his own equipment.
Allowing time for cleaning equipment after use.
Checking electrical equipment regularly.
Training operatives in cleaning procedures.
Instituting a method of stock control including stores ledger cards, bin cards and stores requisition forms.
Operating the 'First In First Out' (FIFO) system of stock control for materials.
Keeping the store clean, dry and tidy.
Teaching cleaners which chemicals must not be mixed together.
Providing a service chart for equipment.
Ensuring that poisons are locked in a cupboard.
Arranging a definite time for issuing materials.
Allowing issue on requisition forms only.
Keeping the store at a temperature above freezing if emulsion polishes are stored.
Auditing stock periodically.
Instructing cleaners in the meaning of 'Flammable', 'Caution' and other signs on labels.

Security

Most cleaning is carried out outside normal working hours with the result that cleaners are sometimes the sole occupants of a building. It is the responsibility of the supervisor in charge of the cleaners to ensure that the building is secure whilst cleaning is in progress. One of the first actions of the supervisor should be to find out whether anyone, apart from the cleaners, is present in the building. If there are no permanent security staff on the premises arrangements should be made to enable the supervisor to secure all entrances and exits to the building in order to prevent any unauthorised person from entering.

There will be occasions, once a building has been locked by the supervisor, when a member of the staff may wish to return perhaps because something has been forgotten. If the supervisor does not recognise the person re-entry may be refused and it is, therefore, in the best interest of all if a system is laid down which will enable a bonefide member, of the organisation concerned, to re-enter the building. In some organisations members of staff are issued with passes bearing their photographs. Alternatively it may be necessary to telephone the superior of the person concerned to check the person wishing to re-enter the building does, in fact, work there. In any event some agreed procedure is necessary in the interests of both the supervisor and the person wishing to re-enter the building.

If a break-in is suspected it is strongly recommended that the police are called and that cleaners, particularly elderly ladies, do not attempt to tackle the intruders.

In addition to the security of the building itself the supervisor is also responsible for the security of the contents of the building and of the personal property of the cleaners. With regard to contents some organisations insert a clause in the contract of service of employees to the effect that the employee agrees to be subjected to random searches from time to time. If the cleaners are working in premises containing attractive items, for example a food store or shops selling watches and clocks, it should be realised that cleaners are at risk from the temptation to help themselves to goods which they think may not be missed for some time.

If they are aware that they are liable to be searched on the way out this could act as a sufficient deterrent to prevent them from succumbing to temptation.

The possibility is always present that one cleaner may be tempted to take the property of another cleaner. This can be guarded against by asking cleaners to bring with them only essentials and not an excessive amount of money or other valuable articles. Theft from a colleague is a serious matter and causes both doubt and mistrust amongst all who work together. Prevention is better than cure and if valuables are not brought into the building the problems of possible theft are minimised.

If a superior is to act as a key holder the supervisor is in a position of trust. A key should not, therefore, be handed to another person unless permission from the supervisor's superior is obtained first. This is because it is possible to have a duplicate of the key made often within a very short period of time. If the supervisor suspects that a duplicate does exist this matter should be reported to his superior immediately so that appropriate action, such as changing the lock, can be taken.

The supervisor should also be aware of the action that should be taken in the case of either lost or found property. In the case of lost property a "lost property book" should be in existence and the supervisor should know its whereabouts so that the appropriate entry can be made. Similarly in the case of found property a procedure should be in existence so that the supervisor knows the correct action to take.

If an alarm is present in the building the supervisor should be fully aware of how the alarm operates and which triggering devices are included in the circuit. This knowledge is essential to prevent false alarms being raised with all the resulting inconvenience both to security staff and, possibly, police.

On completion of a cleaning shift it is the responsibility of the supervisor to ensure that the building is left in a safe and secure condition. In the early stages it is recommended that a check list is prepared for the supervisor to ensure that all necessary actions are carried out. Some examples of items that could be included in the check list are as follows:

All taps turned off.
All lights switched off.
Cleaning equipment and materials returned to stores.
Outside doors locked.
Windows shut.
Lifts shut down.
Fire alarm set.
All cleaners present at exit with personal belongings.
Burglar alarm set.

The supervisor should report any irregularity to his superior either immediately at the end of the shift or the following morning depending on the importance and urgency of the irregularity. The supervisor should be aware of what type of event constitutes an "irregularity". Also he should have guide lines concerning which type of event should be reported immediately and which should be reported the following day. In the absence of any instructions to this effect it is the responsibility of the supervisor to make enquiries before starting the job so that the chance of a supervisor being taken by surprise is minimised.

3

PERSONNEL

Staffing

Many large organisations employ a personnel department whose primary function is the engagement, maintenance of personnel records and, when necessary, termination of employment. In small organisations this function is often carried out by the owner, a director or middle manager.

There will, however, be occasions when a supervisor is required either to carry out one of these functions in the absence of his superior or, alternatively, to sit-in at an interview. It is therefore desirable that supervisors should be aware of the purpose and techniques of interviewing.

Selection interview

A cleaning supervisor may, from time to time, be asked to assist in selection of cleaning staff. When interviewing a number of applicants each interview should be carried out on similar lines otherwise it will be extremely difficult to compare the various applicants and arrive at a decision at the end of the interviewing procedure.

The main purposes of a selection interview are to:

Find out about the applicant.

Satisfy the interviewer that the applicant will be able to do the job.

Give the applicant essential information about the job.

An application form, previously completed by the applicant, should give details recording his previous experience and qualifications. Items frequently included in an application form, which are often the criteria by which application form screening is carried out in order to decide who should be asked for interview, are as follows:

Age.

Sex.

Previous employment.

Formal education.

Further training.

Experience.

Outside interests.

Physical health and suitability (e.g. eyesight, hearing etc.)

The above details can be used for comparison purposes with other applicants and at a later date for record purposes. The application form should be examined before the applicant enters the room so that as much as possible is known about the applicant before the interview takes place.

The interviewer must satisfy himself that the applicant will meet the requirements of the job. Some of the main points a supervisor should check are:

Physical condition	– Can the applicant physically carry out the task of a cleaner?
Mental ability	– Is the applicant intelligent enough for the job?
Special aptitudes	– Has the applicant any special aptitudes, qualifications or experience which may make him of particular use?
Attitude	– Does he appear to have the right attitude for the job?

Questions to be asked will vary upon circumstances. As an example some questions an interviewer could ask an applicant for a job as a full time cleaner, if not already included on the application form, could include:

Details of previous employment, last three jobs, types of job and dates.
Are conditions of service, including pay, acceptable?
Attitude towards week-end or shift work?
Willingness to work overtime?
How far has the applicant to travel to work?
Has the applicant a current driving licence?
Does the applicant know any employee?
Is a full or reduced NHI stamp required?
Has the applicant brought any references?

The interviewer should give the applicant details concerning:

The job	– type, method, location, duration, authority and responsibility.
Conditions of service	– pay, breaks, meals and other services, overalls, welfare facilities, promotion prospects and other items included in the general conditions of service of the organisation.

Techniques of interviewing

It is important that the physical conditions are right before interviewing begins. On entering the building applicants should be shown to a receiving area with cloakroom facilities. A comfortable chair should be provided in the interview room. It is important to avoid interruptions. Visitors should be told that interviews are taking place and advised when the interviewer will be available to see them. If a telephone is present the switchboard operator should be asked to hold all calls until after the interviews have finished. When the applicant arrives in the interview room a friendly and relaxed atmosphere should be established whilst maintaining a business-like approach. The applicant should be encouraged to talk about himself and not given a list of details about the job so that he has difficulty in getting a word in. An applicant has only a very limited period of time in which to make an impression and if the interviewer is talking constantly it will be very difficult for either side to arrive at a conclusion at the end of the interview.

The interviewer should not oversell the job otherwise the applicant, on joining, will rapidly become disillusioned. It pays to be honest and to point out the pitfalls and disadvantages as well as the advantages.

The interviewer should ask his questions in a simple and direct manner. Each question should follow logically so that the applicant will not become confused. As few questions as possible should be asked both to conserve time and simplify the evaluation process.

An interviewer can help to establish rapport and confidence by:

Adopting a warm, friendly manner with eye contact and by smiling. (Nervous unprepared interviewers will not make applicants feel relaxed).

Treating the applicant as an equal – eliminating any social bias.

By not dominating or being pompous.

Finding some common interest or experience.

Giving full attention and showing there is plenty of time and that the interviewer knows details of the applicant and has an interest in him.

Adopting his terminology and meeting him on his own ground.

Some basic techniques to raise conversation and to get applicants talking are:

Ask open-ended questions, e.g. what, how, why, where, when, etc. (Not questions which elicit 'yes' or 'no' replies).

Encouragement and follow-up of points made by the applicant.

Use of silence to encourage the applicant to talk.

Pay attention to 'feeling' statements which may give clues regarding the applicants personality, interests, motivation and mental ability.

The interviewer should be aware of inferring too much when questioning and assuming too much when listening to the answers to his questions.

'Four step plan' for interviewing

A 'four step plan' will help an interviewer to organise his thoughts both before and during the interview. Whilst not guaranteeing successful selection this method will at least ensure that important matters are not overlooked.

1. Plan the interview
   Study the job specification if available.
   Prepare a selection and interview plan and rating sheet.
   Study the application form.
2. Commence the interview
   Choose a suitable place to conduct the interview.
   Show courtesy to the applicant.
   Put him at ease at the beginning of the interview.
   Tell the applicant the essential nature of the job and explain briefly the conditions of service.

"Choose a suitable place to conduct the interview"

3. Proceed with the planned questions
   Make a preliminary assessment of the applicant.
   If initially suitable proceed with the interview plan. If not terminate the interview at this point to avoid waste of time.
   Listen attentively to the applicant's replies.
   Ask the applicant for any documents or references.
   Fill in the rating sheet while listening.
4. Conclude the interview
   Encourage questions about the job.
   Make a final assessment of the applicant.
   Give an indication of the decision.
   Leave a favourable impression on the applicant.
   Ask the applicant if he has any other questions.
   Discuss the next course of action.

Typical errors in interviewing

Some errors to be avoided when interviewing applicants are:

Avoid time wasting questions which merely repeat those on the application form.

Avoid superfluous or irrelevant questions because these questions do not advance the evaluation of the applicant.

Avoid questions which imply certain answers as "Do you like working with people?".

Some common errors committed by interviewers and their consequences are:

Error	Consequences
Poor preparation	– Poor strategy – unclear objective, difficult to establish smooth pattern. Unable to rouse applicant's interest.
Asking leading questions	– Prevents applicant 'opening up' prevents 'cues' to further questions; eliminates 'depth'; prevents rapport.
Giving opinions and judgements	– Inhibits openness and further objectivity; may make applicant guarded – irrelevant.
Not pursuing points in depth	– Prevents insight into applicant and checking stated 'facts'.
Asking challenging questions too early	– Prevents rapport; may create anxiety and nervousness with loss of security.
Interviewer talks too much	– Interviewer will feel 'good' – applicant will agree with him and therefore the applicant must be good! Total art of interview is listening and direction with careful open-ended questions. Talking is not control.
Showing bias	– Prevents objectivity and clear assessment. If applicant detects it loss of rapport or facile agreement may result.

25

Not getting at the facts, or wasting time.	– Poor understanding of interview. Interviewer may be 'fooled'. Superficial exchange.
Lack of summaries of points	– Fails to give candidate sense of structure and understanding of him by interviewer.

The above are typical errors and, as can be appreciated, poor conduct of an interview will result in a poor exchange of information. The assessment of an applicant may, therefore, be seriously affected.

It is unlikely that any applicant will prove to be 100% perfect but if the procedures outlined above are followed the chances of obtaining the right person for the job are considerably increased. The benefits of obtaining the right person for the job at the first attempt are many. Perhaps the most important are that the organisation can save a lot of money and the supervisor can be spared a great deal of inconvenience and trouble.

Termination of employment

With regard to termination of employment it is rare for a supervisor to have the authority to dismiss an employee without reference to his superior. In the event of unsatisfactory work by a cleaner a supervisor would normally refer the problem to his superior, for the appropriate warnings to be given, in accordance with the employees conditions of employment.

Hygiene

The standard of hygiene in any building depends on the standard set by the employer and the actions of the employees. The employer normally aims to provide the best possible environment that he can afford. The standard of cleaning and maintenance achieved largely depends on the cleaning supervisor.

Whilst most employees will comply, happily, with rules laid down, as they realise that the rules are for their own benefit, it only requires one individual with bad hygiene habits to make life unpleasant and, perhaps, to spread disease.

Nowhere is hygiene more important than in toilet and wash room areas. Section 10 of the Offices, Shops and Railway Premises Act, 1963, requires that wash room and toilet facilities shall be kept in a clean and orderly condition and all equipment must be clean and properly maintained. The aim of the legislation is to promote healthy conditions and minimise disease.

Personal cleanliness

Cleanliness starts with the individual. A cleaning supervisor should be aware of the standards of personal cleanliness that should be maintained by the cleaners and should set an example by paying particular attention to items on the list below. Attention to these items will not only make life more pleasant but also minimise the possibility of contracting and spreading disease.

Any cuts or scratches should be treated immediately.

Hands and nails should always be washed before eating and after using toilets.

Hair should be shampooed regularly.

Teeth should be cleaned at least twice a day.

All clothing, both outer and under, should be changed regularly and frequently.

Overalls should be worn and should be changed weekly.

Safety shoes or suitable footwear should be worn.

There should be sufficient protective gloves for each person and they should not be interchanged between cleaners.

Lockers should be inspected from time to time to ensure that personal refuse, such as cigarette packets or food, are cleared away and do not become a breeding ground for germs.

Sandwiches should be wrapped in greaseproof paper and properly stored in a personal locker.

Smoking should be permitted only in approved areas.

Cleaners should be encouraged to report at once if they are suffering from any ailment or disease.

"Smoking should be permitted only in approved areas"

Promotion of clean and hygienic environment

A cleaning supervisor must bear in mind that wherever people work closely together there is the danger of a rapid spread of germs for example colds and influenza. One of the main tasks of a cleaning supervisor is to provide a clean and hygienic environment by which is meant an environment where one can live and work in safety from disease. Implied also is that the area should be free from dust, dirt and harmful bacteria.

27

A clean and hygienic environment can be achieved by:

Carrying out a survey of the premises.

Deciding standards required for each area.

Preparing a work schedule for each area including details of machines, materials, labour and times of work.

Preparing a method of working.

Training staff to achieve the required standards.

Checking staff and amending work schedules as required.

Disposal of waste

One of the tasks of a cleaning supervisor is responsibility for the disposal of waste. Waste can be either in liquid or solid form. Solid waste, for example waste paper, dirt and debris from floor sweeping, should be collected and removed to a disposal point designated by the owner or occupier of the building. Removal of this rubbish will normally be carried out by an outside agency for example the local council. A supervisor should, however, ensure that the waste is stored in such a way that it does not blow about in a high wind and can be removed easily and safely when the time comes.

Waste is sometimes stored in plastic bags in which event the necks should be securely tied. Alternatively it may be placed in a metal hopper or "skip" and the lid should be secured to prevent loose items from blowing about.

Liquid waste may be either acidic, alkaline or of a solvent nature. If any of these properties or any other particular characteristic is known the containers should be marked accordingly so that the contents can be disposed of safely by a third party. If the liquid is known to be harmless it may be disposed of by pouring down a sink, or grid, after first obtaining approval from a person with the authority to authorise this method of disposal. Liquids of unknown origin and properties should never be poured down a sink or grid as they may have harmful effects on the effluent or sewerage system. Disposal of non-biodegradable detergents can also cause problems particularly in inland areas and advice should always be obtained before disposal is attempted.

Liaison with others

The cleaning supervisor should be aware that there are many other factors which also influence hygiene and environmental control. A supervisor cannot be an expert in every field of activity and it is essential that he should know the name of the person who should be contacted in the event of a particular problem arising outside the normal scope of his activities. The supervisor should have the name of the person who should be contacted in the event of a problem relating to each of the following activities:

Air conditioning and ventilation plant.

Presence of pests in food store or kitchen areas.

Electrical faults in the wiring or other electrical systems.

Plumbing faults or action that should be taken on finding a burst water pipe.

Nearest fire brigade.

Nearest police station.

Nearest doctor or hospital in the event of an accident.

By adopting a positive attitude a supervisor can make a positive contribution in providing a working environment which is both safer and healthier to those working in the building as well as to the cleaning staff working there.

4

TRAINING

IT has been said that the success of any business is measured by the amount of profit it generates. Profit, in turn, depends upon making the best use of all resources namely manpower, money and materials.

Training enables an organisation to make the best use of manpower. Every job in an organisation needs to be carried out correctly and as efficiently as possible. A job badly done is wasteful of material and time, and, if it has to be repeated, may prove costly.

Everyone needs some form of training even if only for a short time. Efficiency breeds confidence and experience shows that confident employees can handle their jobs better with increased output as a result. A person who has not been trained may become frustrated, lose interest and, perhaps, suffer unnecessary accidents. An employee who is not committed may leave after a short time with the result that added cost may be incurred in recruiting and training a replacement.

Training is a continuous process to meet the needs not only of today but of tomorrow. Training may be:

"On the job" given in the normal work situation by an instructor or supervisor.

"Off the job" away from the normal work situation either within the organisation or away on a course. "Off the job" training is normally only part of the whole training progamme and is usually combined with "On the job" training.

The main responsibility for training is with the top management of an organisation. Training is a tool of management which must be seen not as an end in itself but as a means to an end which is the most profitable use of manpower in the organisation.

The purpose of training a cleaner is to enable him to perform at the same output and quality as an experienced cleaner. Unless the skills of an experienced cleaner are analysed and understood training may be a waste of time.

Benefits of Training to an Employer

Speed of operation.
Fewer mistakes.
Better knowledge of job.
Can produce more in a given time i.e. more efficiency.
Reduces costs.
Reduces accidents.

30

Benefits of Training to an Employee
Satisfaction from doing job correctly.
Greater earnings.
Acceptance by colleagues.
Greater safety to self.
Less effort less fatigue.
Less mental strain.
More settled in job.

Induction training

The aim of an induction training programme is to provide a new employee with information about the company and his job. His duties should be defined as people work better when they know what is expected of them. A new employee should be introduced to his supervisor and fellow employees. He should be shown his working area, the location of the locker room, cafeteria, time-clock and any other areas relating to the job. Safety rules should be explained together with the procedure for reporting accidents. Rules on smoking, drinking, absenteeism and time cards should also be explained. The induction process should be reviewed at periods and checks carried out to ensure that he has a clear understanding of his duties.

Subjects that should be included in an induction training programme for cleaners
It is suggested that the following items are included in an induction training programme for cleaners. They are not listed in order and additional items may be included as required.
Welcome.
Introduce to colleagues.
Show around building.
What the organisation does and how the employee fits in.
History of firm.
To whom responsible and who's who in the management structure.
Company rules and regulations including 'smoking' and 'no smoking' areas.
Conditions of service including absenteeism and sickness.
Issue identification cards or security passes.
Explain duties job description.
Explain present methods.
Explain safety rules (Act of 1974).
Explain any special clothing or equipment, footwear, hair care.
Explain rotas and work schedules if in force.
Fire drill, precautions and escapes.
How to fill in forms, for example time sheets, requisitions etc.
Areas out of bounds.
Demonstration and use of each material and machine.
Standard of work required.
Types of floor.
Accident procedure.

31

First aid procedure.
Trade unions.
Staff welfare and personnel services.
Social activities and clubs.
Personal hygiene no jewellery.
Grievance procedure.
Disposal of waste.
Involve new employee in cleaning a trial area. Correct and repeat if necessary.
Check list for supervisor to check date that operative has completed each part of the induction course.

Principles of instruction

Training should be carried out slowly and every detail of the job should be carefully explained to ensure that each and every member of the class understands fully what is happening.

Before starting to train employees consideration should be given to preparation as follows:

Determine what skills the employee should have.
Assess the time needed to train employees to the required standard.
Prepare a brief description of all the main steps and important key points pertaining to the job.
The trainer should refresh his own memory about all details of the job.
Break down into simple brief steps. If there are more than eight or nine steps two sessions may be required.
Ensure that all tools, equipment and materials are ready for use and in safe working order.
Ensure that a suitable area is available and free from interruption.
Set a good example by having a professional approach and not a casual attitude to the job.

The procedure for training should include the following steps:

The trainee's interest should be stimulated – attitude counts.
The trainee should be put at ease.
Determine any previous knowledge of the job.
Attempt to create enthusiasm for the job.
Sustain his interest.
Prepare instruction material in advance.
Demonstrate the operation, step by step, explaining the need for correct and safe methods.
Let the trainee attempt the operation under the guidance of the instructor.
Continually ask questions to check that the trainee understands what is being demonstrated.
Compliment and encourage the trainee and correct when necessary.
Follow up the training by checking subsequently to ensure that the trainee is performing each operation correctly.

To summarise the six stages in 'how to instruct' are:

Prepare
Tell
Show
Get class to do
Check
Practise
Repeat

The above are sometimes known as the three 'V's' Verbal, Visual, Verify.

There is no substitute for "on the job" instruction. Instruction in a classroom may be useful to give information regarding the proper use of materials and care of equipment. Manual dexterity and muscular co-ordination are best achieved through close observation of the movement of a trained instructor followed by practise and observation. All those watching a demonstration should be asked to go through the method themselves imitating the movement of the instructor and having their mistakes corrected.

Other training methods should be used also. Written instructions, particularly those with diagrams, are extremely effective. These will not only result in more standardised systems but in improved employee morale as well. Meetings, in which cleaners are addressed by their supervisor, have a place in a training programme. They serve to emphasize the importance of a cleaner's work and can be used to highlight any specific cleaning methods or how to correct situations which have led to recurring complaints. Whilst regular meetings can prove advantageous in certain circumstances "on the job" instruction is absolutely vital. There is no substitute for a cleaner being taught his job under actual working conditions.

Settling a new employee

A cleaning supervisor can assist a new employee to settle into a job, apart from the use of a formal induction training programme, by making the new employee feel wanted. The supervisor should pay particular attention to each new employee particularly in the early days. The supervisor should:

Give him responsibility for a specific area.
Visit him frequently.
Settle any queries which may arise.
Ensure his physical needs are met.
Ensure he knows the layout of the building, location of toilets, room for meals and any other necessary places.
Issue him with a locker and give him locker keys.
Issue him with a uniform.
Ensure he works with a reliable colleague.
Give him praise and encouragement.
When in his presence be cheerful and smile.
Include him in discussions particularly at break times
Attempt to create in him a feeling of belonging.

Advise him of his responsibility for his personal property.

Explain duty rota and work schedule details.

Ensure he has company for all rest and meal breaks.

The sooner a new employee becomes settled in his job the better for both himself and the organisation for which he works. A supervisor can play an important part in helping him to settle and attention to this matter can pay handsome dividends.

"When in his presence be cheerful and smile"

Appraisals

Appraisal of a subordinate's job performance and career potential with associated salary review is among the hardest of management and supervisory tasks.

It has been shown that ineffective appraisal of job performance can affect job satisfaction and productivity. Also, if decisions on career potential are unacceptable, or if the interview in which they are discussed is unsatisfying for the subordinate, the individual may arrive at the decision that there is no future with this particular organisation and subsequently leave. It is, therefore, important that an appraisal is carried out correctly.

Praise given in an annual interview devoted to explaining a salary decision by a senior has little effect, if any, on work performance. Criticism provokes defensive action. Appraisal of job performance appears to work best when carried out at a time different from that of salary review. It is likely to be most useful when linked to an employee's contribution to the organisation or unit objectives and when based on a number of discussions of this kind spaced throughout the year.

Aims of appraisal

The aims of appraisal are:–

To give a true unbiased measurement of a person's performance relative to job specification.

To assess future potential.

Salary review related to merit. Although salary review is influenced by a person's current performance and potential it is strongly recommended that salary should not be considered during an appraisal interview. Any salary negotiations should be conducted separately at a later date.

To give staff an opportunity to recognise and correct faults.

To let staff know how well they are getting on in their jobs.

Development of employee.

To motivate staff.

To improve their effectiveness.

Benefits of appraisal

An appraisal can benefit both the employer and employee. Some of the main benefits are:

For the employer

Improved motivation, morale and commitment resulting from improvement in the planning of the individual's future work.

Improved communication between management and subordinates.

Provides information to management concerning succession and manpower planning with particular reference to transfers to other departments or finding management and supervisory potential.

Gives management an indication of the effectiveness of previous training and development of the individual. Also identifies further training and development requirements.

Provides the management with information for use at a subsequent salary review.

Indicates to management that the person concerned is in the right job.

Lets the employee know that he is recognised as an individual instead of just a cog in a large machine.

Enables management to discover the attitude of the staff to their jobs.

Enables management to ascertain whether motivation is needed and to what extent.

Enables management to gain knowledge of how the organisation appears to members of the staff and may give some indication of reasons for absenteeism and labour turnover if the appraisal shows that widespread dissatisfaction is evident.

For the employee

Gives the individual an opportunity for greater participation in planning future work.

Gives a better understanding of what is involved in the job and the results expected.

Gives an opportunity to find and correct any weaknesses.

Enables an employee to understand achievements and progress he has made.

Indicates that superiors appreciate contributions made and have the employee's welfare in mind.

Gives the employee an opportunity to agree action, for example training, for greater development.

Gives an opportunity to explore greater responsibilities leading to increased achievement.

Gives increased satisfaction and effectiveness through better motivation.

Assists to sort out any problems.

Gives the employee an opportunity to suggest any improvements which may benefit him or the organisation.

Appraisal of current performance

An appraisal of current performance should be carried out by reviewing the responsibilities with a subjective general rating sometimes with a rating of each responsibility. Also by a review of agreed targets and the agreeing of new targets.

These targets may be either quantitative or qualitative. An example of a quantitative target is to reduce wastage of detergents and polishes, by 5%, over a period of three months. An example of a qualitative target might be to ensure that the standard of cleaning of a particular area is raised to such a level that no complaints will be made during a period of, perhaps, three months. Alternatively a target could be that mops and mopping equipment will be kept clean and serviceable with the aim of not replacing any over a period of, perhaps, three months. Note that in the examples given the period of three months is one that is achieveable, within the foreseeable future, not being either vague or open ended when it might become meaningless.

Appraisal of potential

An appraisal of potential is achieved by projecting past performance into the future. This is achieved by an objective analysis of the requirements of the next job as to where it is different from the present job and by measuring the skills and abilities of the person against these demands.

The personal qualities of the individual may be considered if they are likely to affect the overall result.

The appraisal interview

The appraisal interview is inevitably complicated by the fact that the superior has a main influence on the job performance of his subordinates. Many organisations overcome this by arranging for the subordinate to set the standards on which his performance is to be judged.

Senior and subordinate jointly agree the latter's targets, sometimes quantifiable as described above, with dates for completion.

Interviews use these targets as an agenda and set new targets for the next period generally three or four months. An annual review, therefore, simply becomes a 'review of reviews'. To summarise an appraisal of job performance requires a continuous living relationship between seniors and subordinates with two-way communication and not merely a routine mechanical procedure at set intervals.

Every subordinate should know and agree with his superior what is expected of him and this is the standard that should be used when assessing his job performance.

Preparation by the superior

The superior should study the job description of the subordinate together with information concerning his previous training and development. The superior should also examine the targets previously agreed with the subordinate and assess how he considers the subordinate has performed against them. The superior should also consider what are the major strengths and weaknesses of the subordinate bearing in mind what will be required to meet new targets.

Preparation by the subordinate

The subordinate should examine his job description and ascertain how it relates to his current responsibilities. He should also evaluate his training and development together with performance and make a note of any new plans, targets and ideas he would like discussed at the interview.

The subordinate should be given adequate notice of an appraisal interview to enable him to prepare.

Who should attend the interview

In normal circumstances it is recommended that only the supervisor and subordinate are present. On occasions, however, the manager above the superior may wish to be present but it should be remembered that this could be counter productive in that it might inhibit the subordinate from giving his true assessment of the position as he sees it.

Conducting the interview

An appraisal should be conducted at approximately six-monthly or annual intervals. As the subordinate is bound to be nervous at such an interview it is extremely important to ensure that the right conditions are created at the beginning of the interview. This can be achieved by arranging to hold the meeting in a room, free from interruptions and, preferably, comfortably furnished. The subordinate should be relaxed by general discussion and by reassurance that the interview is intended as a two-way exchange of views. By this method the employee becomes involved in his own appraisal and in agreeing plans for his future. It is also important not to assess items over which the person concerned has no control. If poor results in any particular area become evident any mitigating circumstances should be considered.

Appraisal of performance

The subordinate should be invited to give his own assessment of his performance against previous targets set at the last appraisal interview. The manager should then give his comments and advise him how his standard of work is seen by his superiors. If, during the discussion, it is evident that the superior and subordinate cannot agree on their assessment of the performance attained the situation should be discussed in detail.

After considering previous achievements the conversation should then turn to future targets. Both the subordinate and manager should agree new targets and any help or training required for achieving them. The whole emphasis of this part of the interview should be forward looking rather than criticisms of previous weaknesses.

At no time during the discussion should the performance of an employee be compared with that of one of his colleagues. A friendly helpful approach is most likely to achieve the desired results and the subordinate should be complimented on any work well done.

After the interview it is important that the superior ensures that any training and development, needed by the subordinate, are transmitted to the appropriate person for action.

Appraisal of potential

The superior should discuss the subordinate's hopes and aspirations for the future. The subordinate's needs should be examined together with his suitability for promotion if applicable. It is important that the discussion at this stage should be constructive and should centre on the way in which the subordinate's strengths can be used and developed. Any training needs at this point can be agreed.

It should be remembered that excellent performance at lower levels gives a very limited indication of potential for the hard tasks of a senior man. When evaluating career potential consideration must be given not to the level of achievement so far but to the quality and style of performance; i.e. individual behaviour. This is because with increasing managerial responsibility different skills and qualities are required. When assessing potential superiors should ask themselves questions relating to the subordinate such as: What is his capacity to work under stress; to work against time; to decide on priorities for the day and month; to take rather than evade decisions when evidence is incomplete; to be persistant with problems; to think for oneself and support one's own point of view without arousing hostility in others; to give and accept advice from one's seniors and juniors; to accept delegated responsibility; to develop subordinates by carrying the risks of delegating to them.

Circulation of results

During the appraisal a form should be completed and subsequently signed by those concerned. An example is given at the end of this section.

The completed form should be circulated to the supervisor's immediate superior as it is inadvisable to rely on the judgement of one person particularly for appraisal of potential. A copy of this should be retained by the person conducting the appraisal. Whether a copy of the appraisal should be retained by the subordinate is for each organisation to decide.

Staff appraisal forms

Specimen appraisal forms are shown below dealing with agreed targets for current performance and a review of achievement attained. A typical overall appraisal form is also given together with a simplified alternative which is, perhaps, more appropriate for smaller organisations.

STAFF APPRAISAL FORM

1) Name of Job Holder.

2) Job Title.

3) Name of person conducting the appraisal.

4) Job title of person conducting the appraisal.

5) Date of appraisal.

6) Date of previous appraisal.

7) General performance.

8) **ACHIEVEMENT OF TARGETS**

Description of target	Achievement*	Comments

*A = Achieved with a large margin to spare (quantity, quality or time).
B = Achieved with a significant margin to spare.
C = Achieved perhaps with a small margin to spare.
D = Achieved on target or nearly so.
E = Achieved significantly below target.
F = Achieved substantially below target.

9) New targets.

10) Training and Development.
   a) Specific training suggested.
   b) Additional experience/responsibility suggested.

11) Comments of person assessed.

12) Comments by person immediately superior to writer of assessment report.

ALTERNATIVE
STAFF APPRAISAL FORM

NAME:

AGE: DATE OF BIRTH:

QUALIFICATIONS:

JOB TITLE:

DATE STARTED CURRENT JOB:

JOB GROUP:

PERFORMANCE REPORT: (performance on the job since last report)

ANY SPECIAL TRAINING EITHER ON OR OFF JOB (Since last report)

APPRAISAL:

TRAINING RECOMMENDATIONS:
a) Fresh experience, special projects:
b) Formal Courses:

REPORT DISCUSSED WITH EMPLOYEE:
(by whom and on what date)

REACTION OF EMPLOYEE:

REPORT WRITTEN BY:

DATE: SIGNATURE:

COMMENTS OF IMMEDIATE SUPERIOR TO REPORT WRITER:

DATE: SIGNATURE:

HUMAN AND INDUSTRIAL RELATIONS

The field of human and industrial relations is, perhaps, the most important in any organisation. Taken into account are the individual physical and mental characteristics, abilities, intelligence, temperament and interest of all members. Good relationships are essential if an organisation is to succeed whatever the activity. If relationships are bad there is little chance that the organisation will prosper however knowledgeable individuals may be.

A supervisor has a very important part to play in promoting good relationships between himself, other employees and management. A supervisor can assist in creating good relationships by:

Giving responsibility to his cleaners.
Helping cleaners with their personal problems.
Making sure that safe working practices are followed.
Ensuring that working conditions are as good as possible.
Forwarding cleaners' ideas to management.
Being fair in all dealings with people.
Meeting and talking with each cleaner regularly.
Making allowances for different temperaments.
Ensuring cleaners know what is expected of them in their jobs.
Training cleaners effectively.
Warning cleaners in good time about any changes.
Disciplining his group of cleaners effectively.
Involving cleaners in making decisions where possible.
Giving credit for work well done.
Ensuring that the workplace is clean and tidy.
Anticipating problems and taking action before they arise.
Ensuring equipment is kept in good working order.
Promoting a happy working environment.
Knowing exactly his limits of authority and responsibility.
Having good self control.
Settling grievances promptly so that all concerned are satisfied.

Leadership

Meaning of Leadership

In general terms leadership is the ability to take charge and to lead others to a satisfactory conclusion. A leader should point out the direction for others to follow by setting an example. A good leader will give encouragement to his team and inspire in them a desire to achieve the desired results. A good leader will gain respect from his subordinates by adopting the correct attitude for example by starting ten to fifteen minutes earlier than his cleaners and finishing ten minutes or so afterwards.

The purpose of leadership is to achieve objectives through the activities of others. To accomplish this aim a relationship must be established between supervisors and cleaners which will motivate those carrying out cleaning tasks to act in a positive and constructive way so that each will perform his function to the best possible effect. Attitudes of supervisors broadly fall into three main categories:

Authoritarian:	This approach can range from sheer exploitation to benevolent paternalism.
Democratic:	In which consultation and participation are encouraged.
Laissez Faire:	Allowing staff to cope with the job in the best way they can.

Perhaps a fourth category would be a blend of all three.

Two theories, regarding attitudes to work are:

Theory 'X'	— People dislike work, are lazy, prefer strict direction, are not ambitious and value security above all.
Theory 'Y'	— People get satisfaction from work, will welcome responsibility, will work hard for goals they have helped to set and have unused potential which only needs developing.

The holders of Theory 'X' are likely to have a dictatorial attitude and rarely achieve the best from their staff.

Those agreeing with Theory 'Y' who show confidence in their subordinates, expect good performances and who assist a cleaner to develop his potential ability are most likely to get the desired results.

To inspire a cleaner to identify with the organisation and its aims is of paramount importance and must be the object of good leadership.

Qualities of leadership a supervisor should practice
Show appreciation for a job well done.
Tell people the reasons for doing a job.
Make people feel valued.
Help to create and maintain a pride in the organisation.
Set and require high standards.
Consult employees – listen to their suggestions.
Give cleaners a target at which to aim.
See cleaners are paid fairly.
Ensure cleaners have the correct materials and equipment.
Set a good example.

43

Show patience even under trying conditions.
Have a good knowledge of the job.
Appear neat and tidy at all times.
Show fairness.
Show firmness.
Give clear instructions.
Allow people who like each other to work together if possible.

Motivation

According to Dr. Herzberg avoidance of dissatisfaction is not motivation. Herzberg gave a name to his own theory of motivation – "hygiene". In his terms "hygiene" describes the job environment, the wages, hours and working conditions of the job. It is a supervisor's job to "clean up this environment" if he wants to avoid dissatisfaction on the part of employees. Avoidance is not, however, motivation.

As Herzberg states "Good working conditions are like water purification or rubbish collection. These don't make people healthy they keep them from being unhealthy. Similarly good working conditions don't make people happy they keep them from being unhappy".

As most supervisors know the management of hygiene is a never ending problem. The satisfaction that comes from a salary increase, for example, is short-lived. Nevertheless it is important that hygiene is kept at an acceptable level or dissatisfaction will interfere with output. Hygiene however cannot motivate employees.

Motivation, in Herzberg's terms, comes from an internal stimulus resulting not from the way the employee is treated but by the way his ability is recognised and used. It results from the job content not the job environment. Thus it is necessary to "enrich each job to provide responsibility", opportunity for achievement, recognition for achievement and individual growth. These are the internal motivators which ensure high level peformance on the job.

The management of motivated employees is vastly different from traditional methods of management. Essentially it means giving both the carrot and the stick. It eliminates many of the accepted control systems and reward systems as a means of increasing productivity. It requires a high order of leadership on the part of supervisors and, in short, is not easy.

If we are to have efficiency in an organisation, Herzberg states, supervision will have to adopt these new concepts and techniques. Successful organisations of the future will be the ones which make full use of each employees maximum ability and this can only be done through internal motivation.

Team spirit

One of the jobs of a supervisor is to create and foster a team spirit amongst his cleaners. Creation of a team spirit is an essential part of any supervisor's job and a good team spirit amongst cleaners is to be prized.

Some of the ways by which a supervisor can promote a team spirit in his department are:

Show appreciation for a job well done.
Help create and maintain a pride in the organisation and team.
Require high standards.
Consult staff and listen to suggestions.
Ensure staff are fairly treated.
Ensure staff have correct equipment and materials.
Set a good example.
Investigate grievances immediately.
Know cleaners strengths and weaknesses.
Ensure all know exactly what they have to do.
Rotate work so that dirty jobs are shared and that no favouritism is shown.
Promote good working conditions.
Keep staff informed of happenings.

Mentioned above is the point that grievances should be investigated immediately. If grievances are allowed to fester they can have a demoralising effect not only on the person concerned but on his colleagues. Grievances should be dealt with as soon as they occur, either by the supervisor himself or by higher management, as appropriate.

Effects on performance which can result from an employee suffering a grievance:

Reduced output.
Poor quality work.
Resignation to situation.
More supervision needed.
Susceptibility to accidents.
Depression or poor morale.
Intimidating other workers.
Bad timekeeping.
Undermining the team spirit.
Reducing morale of fellow workers.

Change

We live in a rapidly changing world. We must adapt to change to enable us to move with the times. People resist change largely because of sheer laziness as it is easier to continue as one has done in the past and also because of fear. Fear of being made to feel inadequate, of losing one's job or, perhaps, of being replaced by a machine. Numerous instances are known of equipment and machinery being bought to assist in cleaning operations only to find that after a comparatively short time the new machines and equipment are pushed into cupboards, or hidden away, never to be used again. At best machinery may be transferred to another department or sold at a loss. At worst the machine may be deliberately sabotaged, sometimes repeatedly, to ensure that it is not usable.

Technological advances in the cleaning industry have been many, and rapid, in recent years. Whilst the more progressive organisations have managed to keep abreast of developments many have not attempted to change their ways at all.

Even today, with all the modern cleaning equipment and machines available on the market, cleaning staff are still seen on their hands and knees scrubbing floors with soap and water. Whilst the idiosyncrasies of certain people might well have been acceptable a few years ago, when the cost of labour was relatively low, organisations are more cost conscious today. The situation has now changed to such an extent that only the most efficient organisations, employing labour to the utmost advantage, are likely to survive the intense competition that exists in the market at present. State owned organisations are under pressure to reduce costs and this situation is likely to continue. With the slow transfer of wealth from the richer western nations to the developing nations of the third world the pressure on management and supervision to maintain costs at an absolute minimum are liable to remain almost indefinitely.

It is therefore increasingly important that modern technology and techniques, where they can be shown to improve efficiency, are adopted.

That there should be resistance to change, particularly by the elderly, is only to be expected. A resistance to change is inbred in almost everyone. This applies equally to domestic circumstances as to industrial ones. It is easy to fall into a familiar routine and pattern of work and it requires effort to change. Also the very fact that a new piece of equipment, material or method has been developed implies that the old system, which may have been used for many years, was, in fact, incorrect. This is often unacceptable to some people who may strongly resent any criticism. Again whilst the present methods are known, and have been used, perhaps, for some time, new methods are unknown and most people have a certain, if not fear, at least, apprehension of the unknown.

For example a cleaning unit that has for many years simply used mops and buckets for maintaining an area of floor may be introduced to a scrubber/polishing machine which is going to do the job for them more quickly and easily. It will be understandable for the group to resent the arrival of this machine as, firstly, they may not understand how to use it properly and may also resent appearing to be ignorant. They may recognise, also, that if the machine is adopted it might well replace one or more of their jobs. In that event adoption of the machine may simply mean working themselves out of a job. This is hardly likely to endear them to a change of method. Also adoption of the machine may well mean that instead of the unit comprising of perhaps three or four people it might mean that only two are employed in this particular area. The result could be that the unit could be split into two units instead of one which might mean that the whole point of going out to work, which may be meeting people and having an opportunity to talk, is defeated.

The factors mentioned above are very real reasons why people will resist change. Changes must, however, take place if the cleaning industry is to progress. No organisation can afford to stand still. To do so, particularly when other organisations are advancing at a rapid rate, is equivalent to moving backwards. It is inevitable that changes will take place and, despite the resistance of people to change, some changes must be introduced. The question, therefore, is how to persuade people to accept change. Whether changes are accepted, or rejected, will depend to a very large extent on the way this problem is approached.

When change is contemplated the first thing anyone wishes to know is how he will be affected. People must, therefore, be persuaded to accept change and change must not be forced onto people. If a cleaner is instructed to carry out a certain operation by different methods to the one he is normally used to there is little chance of success. It is difficult to persuade people to accept change if they do not wish to do so. The idea of change must, therefore, be sold, as a product or service is sold, to a customer. Any change should be brought about over a period of time. This will allow those concerned to slowly assimilate any new ideas and, hopefully, to accept them as common place once they have got used to them.

How to introduce change

As soon as a change is contemplated give all those concerned the reasons for the change.

Give as much prior notice as possible.

Make a list of the benefits that can be expected from the change both with regard to the organisation and to the personnel concerned.

When selling the benefits to those concerned try to be as realistic as possible concerning the advantages that both, the organisation and those concerned, will gain. Exaggerated claims tend to detract from the credibility of the person concerned if the claims subsequently prove to be false.

Invite those involved to comment on the contemplated change. They might, indeed, be able to make some real contribution either towards improving the change or in some other way.

Consider whether it is possible to introduce change on a progressive basis, rather than all at once, if a lot of change is involved. The benefits of a gradual change must always be compared with those to be gained from a sudden change.

Try and get personnel concerned to contribute towards the change themselves thereby obtaining their tacit approval by involving themselves in the operation.

If other organisations have carried out similar changes try and show how they have benefited.

If the work force continues to hold strong objections obtain approval for a trial period to see how the changes work. During the trial period the operation should be very carefully monitored to ensure that the change produces the desired results.

Provided the proposed change will stand up to criticism and is, indeed, in the best interest of the organisation persevere with that change.

Once the new changes are in operation they should be monitored to ensure that the old system is not re-adopted.

Absenteeism and labour turnover

One of the problems frequently faced by a cleaning supervisor is that of absenteeism and labour turnover.

"Absenteeism" can be defined as time lost other than that granted by management or due to industrial disputes.

The term absenteeism means different things to different people. It will be used in this context to cover all absence of one day or more when an employee is normally expected to attend work excluding that granted by management or due to holidays or an official union dispute. It has been found that absenteeism is normally attributed to illness or injury and this normally accounts for more than 3/4 of all industrial absenteeism. Absenteeism can prove extremely costly. If a company has 1,000 employees working a 250-day year 5% absenteeism will mean that 12,500 work days are lost. If an estimate of the cost of a day's absence is as low as £5 5% absence will cost 12,500 x 5 = £62,500 per year!

Absent cleaners mean more work for those who attend and frequently one result of absenteeism is that the supervisor must stand in for the absent cleaner with the result that supervision overall suffers. No supervisor can carry out his duties effectively if he is fully involved in carrying out a cleaning function himself. Alternatively cleaners may be asked to carry out additional work with the result that standards may suffer and the job may be skimped. In either event the results may not be of the standard required so that both the work and cleaning staff suffer.

Frequent turnover of staff is both disruptive and costly. The actual cost of engaging, training and preparing a cleaner to carry out cleaning duties can prove quite considerable. It is clearly in the interest of the supervisor to ensure that once staff are trained they are retained for as long as possible. Some of the reasons why organisations in the cleaning industry suffer from absenteeism and labour turnover are as follows:

Factors relating to the job:

Too many bosses – bad management.
Lack of supervision.
Lack of training and poor follow-up.
Lack of status.
Lack of job satisfaction – considers job not worth while.
Considers that the work is degrading – low in the social scale.
Better career prospects elsewhere.
Lack of equipment and materials.

Absence of a canteen.
Poor relationship with trade unions.
Working surroundings are not what he was led to believe at the interview.
Unsocial hours – very early, very late or week-ends.
Poor organisation.
Lack of communication.
Absence of planning.
Unfair discipline.
Slight promotion prospects.
Work unfairly allocated.
Too much work.
Introduction of new machines and methods.
Absence of welfare facilities – poor washroom/locker room.
Job oversold at interview.
Boredom with repetitive work.
Bad work schedules.
Poor relations between management and cleaning staff.
Disputes and arguments between cleaning staff.
Wrong equipment and methods resulting in back ache.

"Disputes and arguments between cleaning staff"

Factors relating to the cleaner:

Cleaner feels he does not belong – different colour or race.
Uncomfortable working conditions – too hot or too cold, too dark or too damp.
Does not fit in socially with other cleaners.
Grievance not settled.
Unacceptably low pay.
Lazy temperament.

49

Morale low.
Absence of a sense of responsibility.
Overslept.
Genuine sickness.
Does not like and cannot work with colleagues.
Hours do not suit family arrangements.

Other factors include:
Cleaning is often regarded as a short-term answer to a pressing financial need.
A generous sick pay scheme is sometimes abused by unscrupulous cleaners.
The job may be used as a stop gap or as a step to better things.
The cleaner may be tempted by other attractions for example a football match.
Poor travel facilities to work.
Bad weather conditions.
If a cleaner is receiving good pay he may consider a day off can be afforded.
Absence of incentives to attend.
Seasonal work, for example strawberry picking, may prove more attractive for short periods.
Poor selection resulting in unsuitable staff in the first instance.

Some factors associated with absenteeism are:

Younger employees tend to take frequent but shorter periods of absence than older people. Some cleaners may take more time off than others because of family circumstances. Also those travelling a distance are found to take 20% more time off than those living locally. People arriving to work by car are more likely to take a day off.

How to minimise absenteeism and labour turnover

The cleaning supervisor can assist to minimise absenteeism and labour turnover by taking the following action:
Ensuring, as far as possible, that selection methods are adequate.
Giving adequate induction and on-the-job training.
Attempting job enrichment to give job satisfaction by setting standards and training staff to achieve them.
Delegating jobs as far as possible to give the cleaner a sense of responsibility.
Giving adequate supervision.
Attempting to improve the status of cleaners by providing clean overalls, up-to-date machinery, equipment and materials.
Trying to provide as attractive working conditions as possible.
Ensuring materials are available when required.
Issuing each cleaner with an up-to-date job description.
Making operatives personally responsible for an area.

Initially working with cleaners to get them involved in their work.

Setting a good example.

Listening to cleaners ideas and discussing their recommendations for improvements with them.

Giving encouragement and praise when due.

Trying to make cleaners proud of their achievements.

Praising in public reprimanding in private.

Issuing any duty rotas well in advance.

Being sure duty rotas are fair.

Changing the dirty and unpleasant jobs around from time to time.

Allocating overtime fairly.

Disciplining all cleaners equally and fairly.

Disciplining a persistant absentee.

Being approachable, fair and loyal to both management and staff.

Keeping staff informed of changes.

Showing staff one cares by taking an interest in both work and home activities.

Showing staff that prospects of promotion are available.

Communicating well both up and down.

Taking immediate action re grievances.

Ensuring all cleaners know that in a small team absenteeism lets colleagues down.

Keeping records of absenteeism and checking with other departments to see if a common pattern emerges.

Adjusting hours to suit cleaners if possible.

One way a supervisor can assist in tackling absenteeism is to monitor the attendance records of new cleaners during their first six months. At the end of the fourth or fifth month the cleaner's attendance record should be studied and a decision made as to whether the record is satisfactory or not. If not recommendations should be put to the appropriate manager to consider whether employment should be extended beyond the six months period.

A supervisor should always be aware that the quality of management in general, and of his action as a supervisor in particular, frequently has a very significant effect on the level of absenteeism and labour turnover in his department.

Younger versus older cleaners

It is often the policy of organisations to employ younger, rather than older, people particularly as cleaners. This is because younger people are generally considered to be stronger physically, healthier and more alert and adaptable than older people. A fully trained young person will be able to serve an organisation for a considerably longer period of time than an old person who may have only a few years to serve before retirement. A younger person could also be expected to handle heavy buckets and pieces of electrical/mechanical equipment easier than an older person. Young people are also generally more

51

receptive to new ideas and to change.

There are, however, advantages an employer could expect to gain by employing an older person in preference to a younger one. Perhaps the main advantages are:

Experience leading to a greater awareness of the job.

Knowledge of the job equipment and materials involved.

A more responsible attitude often resulting in better work.

A more conscientious approach to the job.

Greater loyalty – less likely to be on the lookout for another more glamorous job.

Generally a better time keeping record.

Less susceptible to distractions.

Greater awareness of safety standards leading to fewer accidents.

Less absenteeism because of a more responsible attitude.

Greater stability in outlook and performance.

Often a steadying influence on younger colleagues.

Jobs sometimes taken for social reasons.

Older people are often more tolerant and easier to work with.

It should be remembered that some people take cleaning jobs to fulfil a specific objective for example to earn additional money for Christmas or summer holidays. A supervisor should be aware of whether any cleaners in his department are in this category so that arrangements can be made regarding replacements in good time.

Employment legislation

Whilst a cleaning supervisor would not be expected to have a detailed knowledge of the law and industrial legislation relating to activities in the cleaning industry he should have a working knowledge of each of the items detailed below so that in the event of a query he would be aware of where an answer could be found.

Contracts of Employment Act 1972.

Race Relations Act 1976.

Sex Discrimination Act 1975.

Equal Pay Act 1970.

Health & Safety At Work etc. Act 1974.

Factories Act 1961.

Offices, Shops and Railways Premises Act 1963.

COSHH Regulations 1988.

Employment Protection (Consolidation)Act 1978

Employment Acts 1980 and 1982

Employment Protection (Part-time Employees) Regulations 1995

CHIP Regulations 1993

EC Working Time Directive (93/104/EC), which came into force on 1.10.1998

A supervisor should also be aware of the basic benefits and qualifying requirements in connection with employment under current social security legislation.

6

COMMUNICATIONS

PERHAPS the most important part of a supervisor's job is to achieve results through people. A supervisor's effectiveness depends on putting his ideas across clearly and in a way that will ensure that the desired results are achieved. Whilst the management of many organisations would prefer to communicate directly with the cleaners, in large organisations this is not possible. Two, three or more levels of management may come between the general manager and his workforce.

Some organisations communicate with their cleaners by means of:

A house journal.

Notices.

Periodic visits.

Periodic letters to all members of staff.

Management cannot, however, discuss the items detailed above with cleaners and unless the information is very clearly presented the wrong message easily could be read "between the lines". All the above are simply aids to communication. They are generally better than no communication at all but are no substitute for a question and answer session or a discussion on the information given. The supervisor is the direct personal link between the cleaning operatives and management and has a clear responsibility for this function. A cleaning supervisor must communicate in two directions both "downwards" to the cleaning operatives and "upwards" to management.

A supervisor is communicating when he is talking and listening. To communicate effectively it is necessary for him to have an understanding of those things that get in the way when he tries to impart his ideas to another. What are these hindrances to giving and receiving information? Why is it that some people do not understand what the speaker is trying to tell them and why do they assume meanings the speaker never intended? It is up to the supervisor to make himself understood and to find out what the other person means. Most supervisors will find the subject of communication a profitable one to study.

Almost everything a supervisor does involves communicating in one way or another. For example a supervisor is communicating when he is directing, ordering, instructing, delegating or rendering an account of his activities.

The field of communication is very wide and takes in all the ways by which men try to impart their ideas to others. Examples are:

Spoken words.

Written words

Pictures.

Gestures.

In a small department communications are generally at a more personal level namely face to face. In a larger department communications may be by telephone, letter, memoranda, bulletins or by notices in pay envelopes etc.

A supervisor who is not achieving results through people should ask himself whether he is communicating effectively. Both listening and speaking are extremely important activities for any supervisor and good supervisors are generally those who master the art of both listening and speaking. To improve both of these arts a supervisor should ask himself the following questions:

Listening

Are you waiting impatiently for the other fellow to stop talking so that you can start?

Are you in such a hurry to offer a solution that you do not wait to hear the problem?

Are you listening only for what you would like to hear?

Do emotional blocks get in the way of your listening?

Do your prejudices interfere with your listening?

Do your thoughts wander while the other person is talking?

Are you memorising details instead of grasping the main points?

Do you stop listening when the subject matter gets difficult?

Do you have a negative attitude while listening?

Do you just pretend to listen?

Do you put yourself in the speaker's place to try to understand what makes him say that?

Do you take into account that you and the speaker may not be discussing the same topic?

Are you alert for misunderstandings which could arise because the words do not mean the same to you as they do to the speaker?

Do you try to find out what an argument is about – a real difference of opinion or just a matter of stating the problem differently?

Speaking

Are you careful to watch for signs of misunderstandings in your listener?

Do you choose words that fit the listener's intelligence and background?

Do you think out directions before giving them?

Do you break down orders into small enough packages?

If a subordinate does not ask questions about a new idea you are presenting do you assume that he understands it?

Do you speak distinctly?

Do you control distractions as far as possible?

Do you tidy up your thoughts before speaking so that you will not ramble?

Do you put the listener at ease?

Do you encourage questions?

Do you assume that you know what the other fellow has in mind or do you ask questions to find out?

Do you distinguish between facts and opinions?

Do you stiffen up the opposition by contradicting his statements?
Do you influence your subordinates to be "yes men"?

Results of poor communication on cleaners

Consider the effects on cleaners working for a supervisor who is a poor communicator. These could include:

Frustration and resentment.
Low morale.
Misunderstanding of instructions.
An increase in accident rate.
Disinterest leading to absenteeism and lateness.
Lowering of performance.
Lowering of discipline.
May cause disputes.
Wrong use of materials and equipment.
Wasted time – longer breaks.
Poor co-operation with management.
Little regard for the organisation's objectives and targets.
Poor co-operation with each other.
Staff may bypass supervisor and go straight to management.
Less enthusiasm.
More grievances.
Less respect for supervisor.
No feeling of pride in the organisation.

Receiving instruction from management

To be able to pass instructions from management to cleaners it is necessary for the supervisor to understand exactly what is required. Whilst many members of management imagine that they are communicating clearly frequently this is not the case. Some of the major faults and omissions which supervisors find when they are receiving orders from their immediate superiors are:

Instructions vague.
Not clearly presented.
Too hurried.
Too detailed to be practical.
Not complete enough.
Too many instructions at one time.
Imprecise.

A supervisor should not simply accept vague instructions and leave a meeting feeling that any one of the above items applies. If any doubt or questions arise during the meeting these should be voiced so that at the end of the meeting the supervisor is clear in his own mind exactly what is required of him.

Communicating "downwards"

One of the jobs of a cleaning supervisor is to interpret management policy decisions to cleaning operatives. If the supervisor disagrees with policy the supervisor may say so to the management but this disagreement should not be communicated to cleaning operatives. The supervisor is bound to support his management's decision in public.

A supervisor must pass on sufficient information about the job, department and company to enable cleaners to work intelligently and with enthusiasm.

Most supervisors communicate with cleaning operatives either individually at the cleaner's place of work or at informal or formal meetings where a number of cleaners is gathered. Such a meeting may be convened to discuss changes in methods of working or to introduce new equipment or materials. Only on rare occasions will a supervisor need to communicate downwards by means of a written communication.

As most communicating with cleaners is in a "face to face" situation knowledge of how to communicate verbally is essential.

One famous gentleman, noted for his ability to communicate but not for his academic achievements, once was asked how it was that he managed to get his message across so well to those listening. He replied "First I tells them what I am going to tell them, then I tells them then I tells them what I told them". Presentation, often saying the same thing in a number of different ways, is frequently necessary to get a message across.

How to give orders

Since the directing of subordinates is an essential part of supervising the supervisor should remember and observe these suggestions for giving orders effectively.

Have in mind a clear picture of the order that is to be given: know the 'what' of the order.

Keep in mind the specific purpose to be achieved through having the orders carried out: know the 'why' of the order.

Fit the order to the receiver.

1. Know the extent of his competence.
2. Remember his strong and weak points in previous situations.
3. Know his attitudes.
4. Know how to motivate him.

Express the order in concrete terms and if necessary use examples when explaining.

Make sure the recipient understands the "what" and "why" of the order.

Let the receiver know what is expected in quantity and quality: how much is to be done and know how well it is to be done.

Spot check while the order is being carried out. If the job is going wrong because of misunderstandings find and repair the weak spot in communicating.

To ensure that instructions are being carried out it is necessary for a supervisor to make planned checks on various points. Checks should continue until the supervisor is satisfied that the job is being done correctly.

Meetings

Before any meeting a supervisor should ensure that the meeting is well planned and that the message to be communicated can be put across in the time available. Any aids for example an overhead slide cine-projector, television set and video cassette recorder, cassettes, cleaning machinery, equipment or materials should be checked, to ensure that they are in working order, before the meeting commences. There is nothing worse than to find in the middle of a meeting that slides cannot be shown because the plug is of the wrong type and will not fit in the socket or that a machine intended for demonstration is broken. A snag such as this can immediately destroy confidence in the presenter.

People learn through their five senses and the more senses they use the quicker they will learn.

An investigation has shown that people learn by:

Seeing	80 per cent
Hearing	14 per cent
Touch	2 per cent
Taste	2 per cent
Smell	2 per cent

Most is learned through seeing and visual aids are therefore most important in any presentation. Notes should be used but not as a script as a person reading continuously from a piece of paper is liable to become boring, with the result that attention may wander, after a comparatively short time.

Most speakers become a little keyed up before a talk. This is good because it means that the speaker cares and by having the adrenalin flowing will perform that little bit better than otherwise. However some speakers become extremely nervous and dread the thought of speaking in public. A simple technique to overcome extreme nervousness is to have the introduction to the subject written down and to take two or three deep breaths immediately before speaking. The deep breaths take oxygen into the system and assist the speaker to relax. Taking the view that the speaker is trying to help the listeners also assists a speaker to relax.

Whilst speaking it is important to use only words which will be understood by those listening. For example if foreign workers are among the audience difficult words should be omitted altogether or if it is essential that they are used they should be explained.

Many speakers tend to address their comments to the front row only because it happens to be nearest. As a result, particularly at a large meeting, those at the back may not hear properly. Any speaker should, therefore, address his remarks to the whole audience ensuring that he speaks sufficiently loudly so that those sitting at the back can hear everything. At question time a speaker frequently falls into the error of accepting a question from the front and answering only that person. The result is that those at the back are not aware of either the content of the question or the answer. At any large meeting, where there is a possibility that people at the back may not have heard the question from a person at the front, the speaker should repeat the question loudly for the benefit of all. Then he should address his answer to the meeting as a whole finishing by asking the questioner whether he is satisfied with the answer. At the end of any meeting the meeting should be formally closed rather than allowing people to drift away.

"Many speakers tend to address . . . the front row only"

Talks should never be allowed to over-run their allotted time. If a break for coffee is set for 10.30 a.m. or lunch 12.30 p.m. those listening will be aware of this fact and concentration and attention is liable to wander as these times approach. It is, therefore, essential that a speaker is aware of the time and either cuts short his presentation, or amplifies it, as necessary, to ensure that the break and finishing times are met. A speaker who finishes early is always preferred to one who over-runs. If the job has been completed in less than the time allowed the meeting should be closed rather than continuing and wasting everyone's time.

Communicating "upwards"

A supervisor's manager will need to know about two main subjects namely the cleaners and their work. In addition to interpreting management's objectives to the cleaners a supervisor should also communicate the feelings, hopes and suggestions of the cleaners to management. This is extremely important and unless a supervisor communicates effectively it is almost impossible for a manager to appreciate how a cleaner sees the situation. When, during a periodic visit by senior management, a manager stops to have an informal chat with a cleaner he, the cleaner, may be somewhat ill at ease and unwilling to discuss anything of significance in any detail. Frequently a cleaner will only answer in monosyllables giving an impression that the sooner the senior manager leaves the better the cleaner will be pleased. Also cleaners often give the answers they think the senior manager would like to hear, rather than illustrate the true situation, especially if the cleaner considers that the senior manager would find it either unpleasant or unacceptable. A cleaner frequently will not want to mention anything which may be derogatory to his superior because they work together whereas the manager may only be seen on rare occasions.

A manager needs to be given sufficient information to ensure that he will never be taken by surprise by his superiors or by another department. A manager needs reports from his cleaning supervisor concerning:

Long term work to be reported at intervals decided by the manager.

Any "exceptional" event which could include completion of a task; any deviation from the main routine, anticipation of a problem likely to occur in the immediate or foreseeable future.

Suggestions or recommendations regarding changes to work methods, materials or equipment.

A supervisor should also report any other information which he may consider his manager should know in order to ensure that the job is run effectively. Such information is often given verbally but there may be an occasion when a written communication, perhaps a letter or report, is necessary.

Written communications

Any written communication must be concise and accurate. One essential is to include all relevant information so that all known facts are available on which to make a decision. If all the facts are not included a decision may be made which may prove to be ineffective or wrong. If all relevant information is included in the first report additional correspondence, to clear up doubtful points or to seek further information before a decision can be made, is avoided.

Writing correctly saves time both for the writer and reader.

The writing of reports, business letters and memoranda has two main objectives:

To enable transactions to be effected without personal contact.

To provide a record of all the significant facts of an event.

Before beginning it is essential to know exactly the message that is to be conveyed and the sequence in which it is to be presented. Memoranda and reports normally should be headed with the subject matter. This is particularly relevant if a communication has already been received with a heading on the top then the same heading should be used in the reply. A heading also should be used if it helps to shorten the communication or if correspondence is beginning which will probably lead to more letters, memoranda or reports on the same subject. Names of those who should receive copies should be agreed in advance with the supervisor's manager. As a general principle anyone affected by the report should be informed. A list of those receiving a copy should be attached to the report so that each recipient knows who has copies.

Regarding layout the opening paragraph should make clear why the communication is being written. If it is in reply to an earlier communication then this fact should be acknowledged.

Next follows the body of the communication which is the most important part. The object is to convey to the mind of the reader, with the least possible effort to him, the information, problem or question which is clear in the mind of the writer. It follows that the communication should be brief but cover all the necessary points. It should also cover the subject in a logical sequence each sub-division of the subject should form a separate paragraph and sentences should be short. If several points require a reply the paragraphs should be numbered. This will help to ensure that no point will be overlooked.

A final paragraph is often not necessary unless to emphasise some point or to sum up the correspondence.

All communications should be signed and dated.

When communicating either verbally or on paper it is important not to use technical jargon or colloquialisms which the listener or reader may not understand. This is particularly important where foreign personnel are concerned. The aim should always be to convey ideas or instructions in the simplest language possible. Generally the simpler the language the less the possibility of misinterpretation. Any hint of ambiguity should be avoided and if an instruction is misinterpreted, or wrongly carried out, the first thought should be as to whether the instruction was clear or whether it could be misinterpreted.

Telephone technique

The technique of using a telephone as a means of communication is a subject in itself. Suffice to mention that anyone answering a telephone should always give the name of the person answering and not just a vague "hello". A person answering a telephone should always have some scrap paper and a pen, or pencil nearby, so that notes can be taken, if necessary, without the additional cost to the person making the 'phone call of a delay whilst the recipient finds some paper and a pencil. Few things are more annoying to a person making a telephone call than a receiver who is not prepared. A supervisor should always have paper and a pen or pencil available when answering a telephone.

When making a telephone call the information to be given should be clear and concise. If necessary facts and figures should be written down before the call is made. Questions that may be asked during the telephone conversation should be anticipated and, if possible, answers should be ready before making the call.

To minimise expense telephone calls should be as brief as possible and unnecessary talk should be omitted altogether.

If the telephone conversation is important it should be confirmed subsequently in writing to ensure that there is no misunderstanding.

7

WORK STUDY

A cleaning supervisor should ask himself constantly questions about the various tasks carried out by his cleaning staff with the aim of improving methods. It has been said that work study is applied common sense. Work study includes method study and work measurement.

Symptoms showing a need for work study frequently include:

Wasted effort.
Pressure of work.
Delays and bottlenecks.
High costs.
Staff discontentment.

Benefits from work study

Benefits that a supervisor can expect to obtain from a work study investigation into the various cleaning tasks for which he is responsible include:

An accurate assessment of labour and materials required for each cleaning task.
An accurate job specification for each cleaner.
More effective planning of cleaning tasks.
A fair allocation of work to each cleaner.
A realistic work target for each cleaner.
Less time for each cleaning task.
Less cleaner fatigue.
Reduced labour costs.
Reduced material costs.

The overall benefits would be a more efficient use of time, labour and materials resulting in a higher standard being achieved with less effort and at a reduced cost.

Definition of work study

Work study has been defined as a term used to embrace the techniques of method study and work measurement which are employed to make a systematic investigation of all the relevant factors in a work situation in order to improve productivity.

"Less cleaner fatigue"

Definition of method study

Method study is the recording, analysis and critical examination of all the methods and movements involved in the performances of any operations and the development of easier and more productive methods and movements.

Definition of work measurement

Work measurement is the application of techniques designed to establish the time for a qualified worker to carry out a specified job at a defined level of performance.

Definition of labour, materials and plant constants

Labour, materials and plant constants can be defined as the assessment of the amount of each required to perform a specified task over a given period as for example one year.

Method study

When considering method study six basic stages are involved:
Select.
Record.
Examine.
Develop.
Install.
Maintain.

Select – Take any cleaning process and ask could the whole job or any part of it be eliminated? This should be the first question because many cleaning tasks may be unnecessary. If, however, the task is necessary take the part which looks as though it could be done more easily, with less effort or in such a way

62

that it would eliminate bottlenecks, and select this for examination first.

Record – An accurate breakdown of the various stages or activities involved in the cleaning process should be noted on paper. The assistance of the cleaner concerned should be invited and his support enlisted to find a better way of doing his cleaning task. Most cleaners are very willing to co-operate and will certainly accept more readily a new method if they have played a part in developing it.

There are five distinct elements involved in any cleaning task:

Element	Activity	Symbol
Operation	Accomplishes or furthers the process	●
Inspection	Verifies quality or quantity	□
Transportation	Moves	→
Delay	Interferences or delays	**D**
Storage	Holds or keeps	▽

When all the operations of any particular cleaning task have been recorded on paper the key operation should be examined.

Examine

Present		Possible future alterations
What is achieved?	Why is it necessary?	What other achievement could be better?
Where is it done?	Why there?	What other place could be better?
Who does it?	Why that person?	What other person could be better?
How is it done?	Why in that way?	What other way could be better?
When is it done?	Why then?	What other time could be better?

Each question should be critically analysed so that all possible improvements are considered.

Develop – Once all options have been critically examined an improved method should be developed. Discussions should be held with all interested parties for example the head caretaker in a school. The new, better method should be compared with the old way to ascertain savings in:

Operations	—	when something is accomplished.
Inspections	—	when quality or quantity is verified.
Transport	—	when movement takes place.
Delays	—	when there is a hold-up.
Storage	—	when something is in store.

When the new method has been agreed it should be incorporated in a report and circulated to all concerned.

Install – The next step, which is perhaps the most difficult, is to install the new method. Timing will depend to a large extent on the changes being made. For example if new equipment is to be used it will be necessary to wait until it has been delivered and cleaners have been trained in its use.

Maintain – The whole purpose of the study will be lost if the new method is not maintained. Periodic checks should be carried out to ensure not only that the new method is employed but also that the conditions which led to the selection of the new method have not changed.

Over a period of several months several minor modifications may be necessary in the light of practical experience and these should be noted and the new method amended accordingly.

Work measurement

Work measurement is concerned with assessing the time allowed for each operation. The method to be used is defined and each job is broken down into its elements. The quantity of work is then measured generally by the use of stop-watches. Ratings and relaxation allowances are then taken into account to arrive at a time allowance for the operation.

The main aims of work measurement are to give a basis for comparing alternative methods, control of labour costs and effective utilisation of plant and equipment.

Job specification

The desirability of providing each cleaner with a job specification has already been mentioned. A job specification can be defined as a detailed description of the individual functions and tasks comprising any particular job. In any cleaning function the starting point would be a careful analysis of the job that is to be done from which a job description then can be based on the information obtained. A job specification is then a product of the job analysis and job description and shows the knowledge, skills, attitudes and standards expected of a job holder in relation to task and task elements. A job specification is essential for the preparation of training programmes. The job specification is the "what" "why" and "how" of the job for training purposes.

Job anyalysis

Job analysis is a process of examining a job and not a document in itself. Job analysis is the essential step in identifying the training needs of a cleaner. The observation, discussion and work study which may be used in the analysis of the job give rise to the job specification. The depth of analysis required will relate to the complexity of the job. One of the points which may come out of the analysis is a confirmation or rewriting of the job description.

Job description

A job description is a document and a statement of the general purpose of the job including the title, function, hours of work, etc., the lines of responsibility, the limits of authority and the general nature of the duties and responsibilities. It does not go into detail for a trainer although it is useful for operating management, a prospective candidate, personnel selection and job evaluation. It highlights duties and does not always break them down into tasks.

A job description can range from little more than a vague title to a clear concise document which is invaluable in focusing the individual supervisor's position, responsibility and key tasks in the organisation. A job description must be prepared in joint consultation between the job holder and his superior. It should be reviewed at due dates at meetings between the supervisor and his superior. At the formal review a discussion should be held with regard to achievement levels when reasons for non-achievement of targets should be examined critically and the plans should be revised as necessary.

The preparation of a job description is not a difficult task but it should be prepared thoroughly.

Whilst many supervisors in the cleaning industry do not, at present, possess job descriptions as management becomes better trained and more enlightened the advantages of supervisors possessing job descriptions are becoming more apparent both to senior management and to the supervisors themselves.

Job procedure

A job procedure is a summary of the main tasks and sub-elements of a job in sequence. It is prepared by taking the duties listed in the job description and putting them into order relating to the jobs to be carried out.

Person specification

A person specification is used for recruitment and selection purposes only and is a specification of the person suitable for filling a job. It usually includes age, appearance, manner, mobility, qualification, abilities, intelligence, motivational factors and adjustment to work situations. It adds up to an ideal profile of the person for the job and includes quantitative standards. It is usually written after the job description and supplemented with information from the job specification. A person specification is a profile of the ideal cleaner for any particular job.

8

BUDGETS AND COST CONTROL

Budget

The word "budget" is defined in the dictionary as "an estimate of revenue and expenditure". Cleaning supervisors are unlikely to become involved in estimating revenue but are likely to be concerned with budgetary control. This means preparing a cost estimate for all activities, measuring actual results against estimate and taking action, where appropriate, to ensure that the estimate is not exceeded. Checks should be carried out at predetermined periods. For a supervisor to effectively control actual costs against a predetermined budget it is essential that information is provided on a regular basis giving accurate information with regard to expenditure on materials, labour, equipment and other items included in the supervisor's budget.

Whilst the preparation of a budget is generally a management task it is frequently the job of a supervisor to ensure that the budget is not exceeded. Organisations vary widely in the amount of information concerning budgetary control that is passed to junior managers and supervisors. Some junior managers and supervisors never see a budget at all whereas other organisations provide cost information to all managers and supervisors and encourage first line supervisors to interpret the information provided and act upon it. It is, of course, important that the recipient of this information should understand what it means and how it can be used to advantage. Some accounting terms frequently used are as follows:

Accounting terms

Direct labour cost:	The gross wages paid to the cleaning staff who work directly on a cleaning job.
Indirect labour cost:	Wages and salaries paid to drivers and other employees who support a cleaning task rather than contribute to to it directly.
Direct material cost:	The value of the materials, for example detergents and polishes, which are used on any particular cleaning job.
Indirect material cost:	The cost of such activities as laundering dust mops. Whilst such an expenditure is essential it should not be classed as a direct material cost.

66

Overhead costs:	These include the indirect labour and indirect material costs from all departments together with the salaries of the management, office staff and the service departments. Also included are other items e.g. rent and rates for the offices.
Variable indirect overheads:	These include items which vary directly with the amount of work carried out as for example oil and lubricants for the cleaning machinery.
Fixed indirect overheads:	These items only vary slightly whatever the level of activity and include such items as replacement lamps for factory lighting. Other examples are rent, rates and depreciation.
Standard costings:	Standard costings relate to budgeting the cost per item, or number of items, under "standard" conditions. Once costs are fixed they become "standard" and are then compared with money spent as each job proceeds. By this method it can readily be ascertained whether a job is being overspent and, if so, in what area of activity. A decision can then be made as to how the situation can be remedied.

Estimating cleaning costs

A junior manager or supervisor may be required on occasions to estimate the cost of cleaning a given area or building. Such an estimate can be achieved by the following method:

The total area should be surveyed noting the area of each room and type of flooring surface together with any special items that should be considered as for example whether the area is open or obstructed. In toilet areas the number of water closets, hand wash basins, urinals and mirrors should be recorded. A cleaning specification for each area then should be prepared. By using a knowledge of the time required to carry out each cleaning operation the total time required to clean any particular area then can be calculated. The frequency of each cleaning operation then is decided and the total time per week required to clean the area calculated in accordance with the following formula:

$$H = \frac{A \times F \times T}{60}$$

Where   H = Number of hours worked per week.
    A = Area in hundreds of square metres.
    F = Frequency of cleaning (i.e. number of times per week).
    T = Time required to carry out a cleaning task in minutes per
    hundred square metres.

For example if it takes 15 minutes to sweep $100m^2$ and this operation is carried out twice per week the number of hours per week required to sweep an unobstructed area of $600m^2$ would be calculated by substituting figures for letters in the above equation as follows:

    A = 6 (i.e. 6 × $100m^2$)
    F = 2 (i.e. cleaned twice per week)
    T = 15 (i.e. 15 minutes to sweep $100m^2$)

Therefore

$$H = \frac{6 \times 2 \times 15}{60} \text{ hours per week}$$

Therefore

$$H = \frac{180}{60} \text{ hours per week}$$

Therefore

$$H = 3 \text{ hours per week}$$

The time required to complete each cleaning task in turn is calculated and all the times added up to arrive at the total work time in hours per week. A figure of between 12½% and 20% is then added to allow for sickness, leave, movement to and from the job and setting up time for cleaning equipment and machinery after each cleaning session.

To arrive at the number of cleaning operatives required the total hours are divided by the number of hours each cleaning operative will work. For example if the total time required to clean a particular building is 300 hours per week and previously it has been decided that this work is to be carried out by part-time cleaners, each working 15 hours per week, the number of cleaners required would be $\frac{300}{15} = 20$.

The direct labour cost is then calculated by multiplying the number of hours per week by the rate that each cleaner will be paid per hour. Then an addition should be made for uniforms, overtime, superannuation, national health insurance, employer's contribution, graduated pension and other relevant costs.

Other costs will include materials, normally between 6 and 10% of the basic wage, together with depreciation on equipment at approximately 12½% per annum. An allowance should be made also for spares and repairs at approximately 2% of basic wages.

It is apparent from the above that costs relating to staff form about 90% of the total cost of cleaning a building and costs relating to cleaning materials, equipment, depreciation, spares and repairs comprise the remaining 10%. As the money spent on cleaning materials, such as polishes, is relatively small it is clearly advisable to purchase good quality materials which will last longer and be more durable than poor quality cheaper materials. Better quality materials need less frequent application and stripping from the floor and thereby reduce the labour content of the job. As labour is by far the most expensive item in any cleaning operation any material or piece of equipment which will reduce the labour content of the job should be given every consideration.

In addition to the above extra time should be allowed for cleaning prestige areas as for example an entrance to an office block or an executive suite of offices.

Factors that should be taken into account when deriving an estimated cost for cleaning a particular area should include:

The standard of cleaning required in each area.
Number of staff required.
Supervision required, including managers, if any.
Wages, pensions, national health insurance and other costs relating to labour.
Types of floor.
Types of furniture, fixtures and fittings.
Area of each floor.
Cleaning equipment and materials required.
Travel facilities to and from the location.
Overheads.
An allowance for depreciation of equipment.
Holiday pay and sick pay allowance.
Storage facilities on site.
Services available i.e. water and electric points.
Accessibility of each floor by stairs or lift.
Hours of access to buildings.
Availability of capital to finance the project.
Availability of capital to finance any equipment required.
Any overalls required by the cleaners.
Any training required by the cleaners.

Costs influenced by a supervisor

In any cleaning operation there are costs that can be influenced directly by a supervisor to a greater or lesser extent. Perhaps the main items are:

Number of cleaners.
Grade of labour i.e. skilled, semi-skilled or unskilled.
Wages paid including overtime if any.
Degree of absenteeism and labour turnover.
Work planning – method of working.

Training and retraining if required.

Checking to ensure the job is done correctly thereby minimising wasted time.

Cost of materials taking into consideration that the cheapest is frequently not the most economic.

Selection of materials ensuring that the right material is used for each job.

Stock control including allocation of the correct amount of materials for each job.

Ensuring minimum waste of materials.

Ensuring that the correct equipment is used for each job and that it is cleaned and serviced regularly to minimise repair and replacement costs.

An awareness of security to minimise theft of materials and ancillary items.

Minimising overheads by ensuring lights are not left on unnecessarily and that heat is not wasted thereby minimising costs of electricity and fuel.

Minimising cost of labour

It has been mentioned that the greatest cost in any cleaning operation is that of labour. A cleaning supervisor can minimise the cost of labour by:

Effective selection of cleaners for the job.

Ensuring cleaners are properly trained.

Issuing work schedules and instruction cards.

Allocating the work evenly.

Using work study techniques if applicable.

Ensuring that cleaners work in accordance with the required methods.

Ensuring that only the required standard of cleanliness is met and that additional work is not wasted in obtaining too high a standard.

Setting goals and monitoring the results of each cleaner.

Ensuring that time is not wasted.

Minimising unnecessary overtime.

Minimising labour turnover and absenteeism.

Developing a team spirit.

Ensuring that the needs of each cleaner are met and job satisfaction obtained.

Keeping morale at a high level.

Motivating each cleaner if possible.

Ensuring cleaners do not get tired.

Ensuring cleaners work a full day.

Having equipment and materials available at the right times and places.

Minimising cost of materials

A cleaning supervisor can minimise the cost of materials by:

Ensuring that the most cost effective materials are used for each job.

Obtaining discounts when purchasing.

Standardising on materials and methods.

Ensuring stores are weatherproof.

Avoiding over-ordering and over-stocking.
Having regard to shelf life for items which deteriorate quickly in storage.
Recording all stores received and issued.
Ensuring that cleaners are trained in the most effective use of materials.
Taking care that labels are not removed.
Ensuring that cleaners replace caps on containers after use.
Operating the first-in first-out system of stock control.
Taking care to avoid spillage.
Ensuring that cleaners use only the correct amount of each material.
Using dispensers if possible.

"Ensuring stores are weatherproof"

Minimising cost of equipment

A cleaning supervisor can minimise the cost of equipment by:
Shopping around to buy at the cheapest price.
Buying machines which will do more than one job if possible.
Buying from a reputable firm.
Ensuring that expensive items are locked up to prevent pilferage.
Ensuring that documentation of machines e.g. date of purchase is properly carried out.
Carrying out preventive maintenance.
Not allowing machines to deteriorate beyond economic repair.
Ensuring that each piece of equipment is properly used.
Reporting any defective equipment.
Ensuring that each piece of equipment is properly stored.
Ensuring that each piece of equipment is maintained in a clean condition.
Ensuring that training is given and that the required results are being obtained for each piece of equipment.
Minimising idle time.

It can be seen from the above that a cleaning supervisor can play a very important part in minimising the costs of any cleaning operation. An effective supervisor can save many thousands of pounds a year thereby making a substantial contribution to his organisation.

9

SAFETY

Legal requirements

The responsibility of a supervisor for the safety of his subordinates and other personnel occupying a building has been highlighted by the Health and Safety at Work etc. Act 1974.

The aim of the Act is to make provision for securing the health, safety and welfare of persons at work, for protecting others against risks to health or safety in connection with the activities of persons at work and for controlling the storage and use and preventing the unlawful acquisition, possession and use of dangerous substances.

Section two of the Act details the duties of employees. This section can be summarised by stating that it shall be the duty of every employer to ensure, so far as is reasonably practicable, the health, safety and welfare at work of all his employees.

Section three describes the duties of employers to persons other than their employees. This section states that it shall be the duty of every employer to ensure that persons not in his employment are not exposed to risks to their health and safety.

Section four details the duties of persons, concerned with premises, to persons other than employees. This has the effect of imposing on such persons duties in relation to those who are not their employees but have access to non-domestic premises as their place of work.

Enforcement

The Health and Safety at Work etc. Act 1974, is enforceable. An inspector can:

Issue a prohibition notice to stop the activity in question if there is a risk of serious personal injury.

Issue an improvement notice to remedy a fault within a specified time.

Prosecute instead of or in addition to serving one of the above notices.

On summary conviction a fine of up to £400 can be imposed. For persistent offenders the penalty can be imprisonment for a period of up to two years.

Non-statutory requirements

Apart from any statutory requirements a supervisor is responsible for the safety of his staff on purely humanitarian grounds. It is the duty of each supervisor to ensure that his staff works in a safe and wholesome environment. Apart from the humanitarian aspect clearly it is extremely inconvenient if staff are absent from work as a result of injury. Absence inevitably means that the work has to be accomplished by other people with the result that those who remain carry an additional burden. Alternatively the standard of work may suffer.

In addition there are the hidden costs of accidents such as compensation paid either by the employer or insurance company together with the loss of time of the supervisor, and others, in investigating an accident and taking steps to prevent a similar occurrence. An additional cost may result from a fall in productivity, which invariably takes place when an accident occurs, apart from the very real financial loss which may befall the person suffering the accident due to loss of earnings.

Whilst many organisations employ a safety officer this person is generally in an advisory capacity and clearly cannot foresee a thousand and one possible trouble spots. All a safety officer can hope to do is to bring to the attention of management and supervisors the likely causes of accidents and any possible preventive measures. Whilst safety talks, meetings, instructions and films may go some way towards providing a safe environment the most important factor is the attitude and approach of each individual from the top to the bottom in the organisation.

A supervisor should lead by example. If his subordinates see that he is conscious of the safety requirements of his job they are far more likely to follow in his footsteps than if he adopts a reckless and cavalier attitude.

It must be stressed that safety officers are in an advisory position and as such have no authority to enforce recommendations. The onus is on the supervisors to instruct and take responsibility for the performance of their personnel.

On occasions unsafe practices or operations are known and reported to management who may take no action for one reason or another. Because of this the practices are repeated until, eventually, an accident takes place. Only then is remedial action taken. In order to prevent an accident in the first place it is essential that those who are aware of a hazardous situation not only report it but also persist in nagging the management concerned until something is done to correct the situation. Whilst management may, on the surface, object to being harassed about a particular safety point they will respect the supervisor concerned for his effort in promoting safety.

Supervisors should pay particular attention to people who are liable to be accident prone at work. Those workers particularly at risk include elderly people and those straight from school. This is because elderly people are generally slow to grasp new ideas and slow to react if an accident should be imminent. If possible older people should be placed in a position where they are not liable to be faced with a hazardous situation.

Young people, just out of school, also are at risk because of their total lack of experience of the industrial way of working and of the equipment and materials in use. Most young people are totally unfamiliar with equipment, materials and machinery used in the cleaning industry and will be unaware of the dangers that can be present when these items are misused.

Many young people work extremely hard and conscientiously but some can be irresponsible and cause accidents to happen simply through their high spirited approach. It is often a good policy to allow a short time for discussion on safety points at periodic meetings.

Good housekeeping

A supervisor should be alert constantly to the necessity of good housekeeping namely general cleanliness throughout the working and welfare areas. A supervisor should be on the look-out for:

Slippery floors caused by oil, grease, water or spillage of any kind. All should be mopped up immediately and the floor made safe.

Holes or bumps in the floor surface which should be reported to the maintenance department for repair.

Equipment left in walkways and gangways creating a hazard. These should be moved to a storage area.

Refuse containers which should be emptied every day.

Oil and paint soaked rags which should be stored in closed safety metal containers.

Cleaners smoking in 'no smoking' areas.

Electric and gas fires which should be switched off before leaving.

Scrap and refuse containers which should be adequate and in their proper places.

"A supervisor should be on the look-out for slippery floors"

Personal protection

Wearing clothing suitable for the job is a major aid to safety. Cleaners should be told why protective clothing is provided and when they ought to wear it. Protective clothing must be properly looked after. Suitable arrangements should be made for storage, cleaning, repair and replacement as necessary. When health and safety are involved the use of correct protective clothing must be enforced. Every year a large number of eye injuries occur. All of these are painful and many are serious leaving the sight permanently damaged. For some jobs goggles or eye shields should be worn. They are essential where acids or strong alkalis are to be used.

In the event of a cleaner accidentally receiving a splash in the eye it should be washed immediately with copious amounts of water using an eye-wash bottle or running tap water. Failing this the face should be plunged into clean water and the eye blinked rapidly. The cleaner should then report to the First-aider for treatment (see First Aid Appendix 1).

Instructions for own cleaners

To comply with the Health and Safety at Work etc. Act 1974 it is the duty of employers to ensure that their own cleaning staff are instructed in the safe handling of materials and equipment.

Safe handling of materials

With regard to materials it is recommended that instruction is given in the following topics to ensure that they are fully understood by all concerned:

Unlabelled materials should not be used. This is because whilst, at best, no harm may result at worst use of an unknown material could result in either an acid or caustic material being spilt onto the skin or onto a surface causing damage.

Manufacturer's instructions should be read carefully before use. The material might be the wrong material resulting in either slippery conditions, damage to the surface or damage to the skin.

Toxic materials should be kept under lock and key. This is particularly important if children, or elderly, sometimes senile people, are liable to take hold of them.

Any material decanted from one container to another should be properly labelled to prevent any possibility of the wrong material being used for a particular job.

Materials should not be mixed together. Whilst mixing an anionic with a cationic detergent neutralises both and renders both items useless and harmless mixing bleach with lavatory powder produces a poisonous gas which has resulted in a number of fatalities.

Where appropriate, protective clothing should be requested by the cleaner for certain tasks. Protective clothing can include aprons, gloves, boots, protective headgear, eye shield and face masks or other apparatus as necessary.

Heavy goods should not be lifted particularly by elderly or infirm cleaners. If heavy goods need to be lifted then either sufficient able bodied staff or mechanical handling equipment should be available.

'No smoking' notices should be provided in those areas where flammable seals or polishes are being used.

Good ventilation should be ensured in those areas where solvent based products are being used.

Staff should be trained in first aid concerning immediate remedy for splashes on the skin or in the eyes. This is to prevent the possibility of dermatitis or skin burns which can be caused by some chemicals.

Any splashes which appear on a floor should be removed immediately. This is to prevent the possibility of either damage to the floor or the liquid on the surface forming a slip hazard.

Any accident or illness to staff must be reported immediately.

Materials should not be left where they can become a hazard as for example in the centre of a busy corridor.

Staff should be technically trained to a competent level to ensure that materials are not misused. For example water based emulsion floor polish should not be applied on top of a floor maintained with a gel cleaner. Floors treated in this way have resulted in slip accidents due to the fact that emulsion polish is prevented from adhering to the floor itself, by the presence of the gel, resulting in very slippery conditions.

Aerosols should be stored in a cool place and disposed of carefully. They must not be disposed of by incineration as the pressure inside the aerosol may result in an explosion if it is heated.

Old cloths should be stored in metal bins rather than wicker waste paper baskets or fibreboard drums. This is because rags soaked in solvent based seal or wax polish can spontaneously ignite causing a fire.

Safe handling of equipment

Instructions that should be given to cleaning staff concerning equipment are many and varied depending on the equipment in use. Where floor polishing/scrubbing machines are in use instructions should include the following:

Before using any new machine or piece of mechanical equipment instruction should be given to operatives concerning its operations and particularly safe handling. If necessary the manufacturer should be approached concerning any specific recommendations to ensure both the safety of the operator and others.

Cables should not be allowed to drag so that they become tangled up with the underneath of the machine. If this should happen the wire may become cut or broken resulting in an electric shock for the operator.

Electric plugs, connections and extension leads to the cable of the machine should not be allowed to rest in water.

Machines should be unplugged when not in use. This is particularly important when children are in the vicinity as they may be tempted to play with an unattended machine and accidentally start it.

Removal of the plug from the socket also prevents the possibility of someone tripping over a taut wire.

When using a machine the cable should be kept behind the operator to avoid the possibility of running over it.

Plugs should be examined frequently for loose wires and cables should be examined for cuts.

Cables should not be pulled taut as this puts a strain on the plug.

Any faulty machines should be reported immediately and a notice attached warning others not to use it.

Any tanks attached to machines, also buckets, should be emptied after use otherwise they may leak and cause a puddle to form resulting in a slip hazard.

Machines and equipment should be stored properly after use.

Sawdust should be emptied from bags attached to sanding machines to prevent fire from spontaneous combustion. Fires have been started by spontaneous combustion after sanding wood floors treated with an oleoresinous seal as an oleoresinous seal can produce highly flammable dust.

Electrical repairs should not be attempted by a cleaner unless he is authorised to do the work.

The supervisor's attention should be directed to any unguarded live wires.

When using any portable electrical equipment the plug should not be forced into a socket that it does not fit.

In any vessel or area where there is danger from a flammable atmosphere only certified flameproof equipment should be used.

When operating a machine with an electric cable stretched across a gangway or corridor the following precautions should be taken:

Markers should be put on the cable.

The cable should be carried overhead if possible.

If the cable is on the floor it should be protected with a cover.

A warning notice should be placed at each end of the corridor.

A trip switch should be fitted which cuts off the machine if the cable is pulled.

Plenty of slack should be present in the cable.

Lifting goods

The largest number of industrial accidents occur during the movement and handling of goods. Many of these accidents, though simple in origin, result in painful disablement and often long periods away from work. General principles of lifting and carrying are simple though not widely appreciated. Correct methods are, however, quickly and easily taught and can be demonstrated without elaborate equipment.

Instruction in good practice could reduce the number of accidents considerably.

Handling methods

Proper hold	— When lifting or pulling rest the palm of the hand against the object and fold your fingers around it.
Straight back	— Many accidents are caused through lifting an object by bending from the hips. Less muscle power is required when handling with the spine straight and legs bent than by lifting the weight by straightening the legs.
Chin in	— The action of raising the top of the head, so that you feel tall and your chin comes in, automatically locks the joints of the spine. This relieves the muscles of a great deal of the work involved in keeping the spine stable thus reducing fatigue in handling.
Proper foot positions	— Balance is extremely important in lifting. Good foot positions ensure that weight is evenly distributed. Feet should be placed approximately 6 inches apart. One foot should always be in advance of the other to assist balance. This foot should point in the direction in which you want to move so that, when you lift, your rear leg automatically follows through.
Arms to body	— Allow your arms to remain as close to your body as possible. This ensures that the object being handled is held close to your centre-line of gravity and there is less strain in neck, shoulder and chest muscles.

Action to ensure safety of building occupants

It is the duty of cleaning staff to ensure the safety of all occupants of a building particularly whilst cleaning is in progress. Action that should be taken by both supervisors and cleaners includes the following:

The area being cleaned should be roped off.

Warning notices should be placed advising that cleaning is in progress.

'Caution Wet Floor' signs should be posted if appropriate.

Cleaning should be avoided during peak movement times if at all possible.

Fire doors, exits, lifts and main doors should be kept clear.

Equipment should not be stored in the main passageways and exits.

Any unattached machinery should be switched off and unplugged.

Machine cables should be laid along side walls or corridors and not allowed to cross the main traffic lanes.

Any damaged floors should be reported immediately.

Materials which could cause slippery conditions should be avoided as for example a solvent wax should not be applied on a terrazzo floor.

Half a corridor should be cleaned at a time, if possible, followed by the other half when the treated area is clean, dry and safe to walk on.

Any flammable materials should be avoided unless the area is adequately ventilated.

'No smoking' signs should be placed in obvious positions if flammable materials are being used.

Cleaning materials and equipment should not be left on the floor particularly if children are present.

Any spillage should be wiped up immediately as this could cause a slip hazard.

If scaffolding is used it should be secured firmly to ensure that it is safe and that there is no danger from objects falling from it.

Lighting should be checked periodically, particularly on staircases, to ensure that no dark patches are present.

Cleaners should be instructed to work quietly as noise is likely to distract people and could cause an accident.

How a supervisor can promote safe working conditions

A supervisor can encourage his cleaners to promote safe working conditions and thereby reduce accidents by:

Setting a good example.

Telling people to do things the 'safe' way and insisting on it.

Checking safety methods on inspection tours.

Advising management of any unsafe practices or items needing attention.

Investigating accidents to prevent recurrences.

Providing protective clothing and insisting it is worn.

Ensuring cleaners wear suitable footwear.

Ensuring lighting is adequate.

Forbidding horseplay particularly by young cleaners.

Watching accident prone people.

Asking for safety suggestions.

Holding safety meetings.

Keeping work areas tidy.

Keeping gangways and exits clear.

Ensuring that transporting and lifting tackle are safe.

Ensuring that equipment and ladders are in good working order and are regularly checked and serviced.

Ensuring that 'Caution Wet Floor' signs are placed at both ends of areas being treated.

Ensuring that all are aware of any safety regulations.

Reporting faults and ensuring that remedial action is taken as for example replacing a broken light on a staircase.

Watching for chafed leads on machinery when in contact with wet floors.

Ensuring that machinery is unplugged when not in use.

Ensuring that staff are not allowed to become overtired.

Treating poisonous or dangerous materials with due care.

Not allowing cleaners to apply polish under mats.

Ensuring that cleaners do not stand on chairs.

Ensuring cleaners lift heavy items correctly.

Not allowing cables to be stretched across corridors.

How a supervisor can promote safety in a storeroom

Some of the methods whereby a supervisor can promote safe working conditions in a storeroom containing both materials and equipment are as follows:

Placing a 'No Smoking' sign prominently in the store.

Allowing only authorised people to enter.

Ensuring that all containers are properly labelled.

Storing flammable items in a separate area.

Providing adequate shelves for keeping materials off the floor.

Providing facilities for the disposal of waste.

Ensuring that all faulty electrical equipment is labelled and repaired.

Ensuring that there is adequate lighting in the store.

Stacking 20 litre drums and fibreboard boxes to an acceptable height.

Putting chocks under 200 litre drums to prevent them from rolling.

Packing shelves safely to ensure nothing can fall off.

Ensuring that heavy items are not lifted above chest height.

Keeping all gangways and passages clear.

Ensuring that any poisonous items are stored in a locked cupboard.

Falls

Falls on the level and on stairs account for most of the 40,000 or so accidents reported to H.M. Chief Inspector of Factories under the category of 'Falls of Persons'. Falls have many causes and contributory factors the most common of which are:

Defective flooring, loose floorboards, cracked concrete, loose tiles, grease, oil or water spilt onto the floor.

Worn out or unsuitable shoes or sandals.

Poor or too bright lighting.

Boxes, cases or other objects in gangways and passages.

Slippery stairs.

Badly constructed scaffolds.

Planks, ladders and ramps not properly placed.

Ladders not on a firm base or placed at the wrong angle – (they should be 1 foot out for every 4 feet up).

An alert supervisor should be on the lookout constantly for the above which should be either corrected on the spot or reported to the appropriate person at the earliest opportunity in writing if necessary.

Slip hazards

It has been said that out of every 100 women workers hurt 17 are injured by falls on the level and on stairs. Also out of every 100 men hurt 16 are injured by falls on the level. In any one year falls disable nearly 26,000 workers.

Slip hazards can arise if floors are maintained wrongly. Safest conditions result from correct floor maintenance. Some of the reasons for slippery floors are:

Application of the wrong type of wax to floors e.g. a solvent based wax on vinyl tiles.

Allowing a build-up of solvent based wax to occur.

Allowing a wax containing silicone, for example furniture polish, to fall onto a floor.

The presence of water, oil, grease or fat on floors.

Allowing a buffable type of polish to remain un-buffed and therefore un-hardened.

Solvent based wax carried over onto a floor treated with a water emulsion floor polish.

A machine brush used for solvent wax being used on water based emulsion floor polish.

A build-up of a gel cleaner.

Application of water emulsion polish on top of a gel cleaner.

Application of a water emulsion polish on top of a solvent based polish or a solvent based polish on top of a water emulsion polish.

The supervisor should be sufficiently well trained to be able to recognise each of the above faults and be able to take action to correct the situation as appropriate.

A record of all accidents, however small, should be kept to prevent similar accidents from taking place and to provide evidence in the event of a claim.

Investigation of a slip accident

However well floors may be prepared and maintained and rigorous supervision exercised it is inevitable that, from time to time, a slip accident will occur. Should the person concerned suffer harm and subsequently be successful in a court action against the owner of the building he may be awarded damages amounting to many thousands of pounds. It is, therefore, in the interests of those responsible for the maintenance of a building that a slip accident is investigated immediately firstly to protect themselves and secondly to prevent another accident from taking place.

The person who slipped and fell should be interviewed and a report prepared. Any witnesses should be interviewed and statements taken.

Once the person who fell has been looked after and any witnesses dealt with, an investigation should take place concerning materials used to maintain the floor together with the method of maintenance. In particular the investigation should be directed towards the actual method of maintenance compared to any written specification which may be in force and whether any build-up of wax or any other items are apparent on the floor. If the accident took place outside the building the atmospheric conditions should also be noted.

To summarise a detailed investigation should be undertaken and a report prepared. The report should be as comprehensive as possible and all relevant facts should be included. This is important because if the injured person should decide to take legal proceedings the case may not appear in court for a period of three to four years after the event. The investigation should include the following:

An interview of the person who fell.

An interview of any witness.

An investigation of any maintenance materials on the floor and the method of maintenance.

Checking the method of maintenance against the written specification.

If outside a building noting the atmospheric conditions, e.g. wet or dry.

Ascertaining whether the person was walking, running or turning quickly.

Investigating the person's shoes for defects.

Was any water or oil present on the soles of the shoes?

Was any wax on the shoes from an adjoining floor?

Was any water or oil present on the floor?

If water was on the floor was a 'Caution Wet Floor' sign placed to warn people?

Attempting to investigate the state of mind of the person. For example was he thinking of other things?

Did the person have an injured or weak leg?

Was the person : very young, old, crippled, blind, handicapped in any other way, drunk, drugged, walking abnormally or off balance perhaps due to carrying one or more objects?

Was the lighting satisfactory?

Have there been any other accidents at the same place?

Slip accident report

Having concluded the investigation a report should then be prepared. The report should include:

Name of person injured.

Home address.

Date of accident.

Time of accident.

Location of accident.

Whether recorded in accident book.

Circumstances of accident.

Were 'Caution Wet Floor' notices in place?

State of shoes.

Statements from any witnesses.

Signature of reporter.

Date of report.

Name of those to whom report was sent.

How to improve slip resistance

Investigations into slip accidents have shown that the chances of a person, walking normally slipping on a floor with a coefficient of friction of 0.4 are one in a million. As solvent based liquid polishes normally have a coefficient of friction of 0.4 and water emulsion floor polishes have coefficients ranging from 0.5 to approximately 0.7 the chances of a person slipping whilst walking on a floor treated with one of these materials is likely to be less than one in a million. Floors treated with water emulsion polishes are generally considerably more slip-resistant than untreated floors. If, therefore, an accident has taken place the cause is more likely to be with the person concerned than with the floor. Indeed investigations have shown that in approximately 95% of slip accidents the cause of the accident was the person concerned rather than the state of the floor. The immediate reaction of management, however, will probably be to ask the supervisor either to remove the existing polish or to substitute a more slip-resistant material. This can be achieved by replacing the present polish by another with a higher coefficient of friction as follows:

Coefficient of friction (approx).

Most slip resistant.
0.7 Dry-bright water emulsion.
0.6 Semi-buffable water emulsion polish.
0.5 Fully-buffable water emulsion polish.
0.4 Solvent-based liquid polish.
0.3 Solvent-based paste polish.
Least slip resistant.

An unsealed wood or cork floor, treated with a solvent based polish, may need to be stripped of polish and sealed before a water emulsion polish is applied.

By changing to a polish with a higher coefficient of friction the slip resistance of a floor can be improved although it should be recognised that in approximately 95% of all slip accidents the cause of the accident is not the polish on the floor.

Safety with ladders

A ladder is one of the most commonly used pieces of equipment and also probably one of the most misused. Using ladders can be fraught with danger. Regrettably there are between 3,000 and 4,000 accidents, involving ladders, in the United Kingdom each year. Of these about 50 prove fatal.

Most accidents are caused by ladders slipping. Even when ladders are inclined at the recommended angle accidents still happen where ladders are unsecured.

Other causes of accidents are:

Ladder slipping sideways at the top.
Ladder too near the vertical.
Over-reaching.
Over-balancing.
Slips on rungs due to muddy or wet footwear.
Ladder resting against a fragile structure which breaks.
Insufficient projection to provide a suitable hand-hold when stepping onto the highest working level.
More than one person occupying a ladder at the same time.
Ladder falling over whilst being placed into position.

Using too short a ladder.

Straddling between a ladder and another foothold.

Being blown off balance whilst carrying large objects in strong winds.

Using ladders horizontally as planks.

Ladder touching live electrical conductors.

Defective ladders.

Ladders should always be carefully inspected before use. Wooden ladders should be examined visually for any obvious defects such as:

Warping.

Cracking.

Splintering of the stiles.

Splintering of the rungs.

Defective fixing of the rungs at the point where they enter the stile.

If the rungs are round each rung should be grasped and an attempt made to rotate each rung in turn. If a rung rotates it is loose and should be mended before the ladder is used.

Metal ladders should be inspected essentially as above but in addition they should be checked with regard to:

Metal corrosion.

Twisting or bending.

Fracture of the metal rungs or stiles.

Fracture at riveting points.

It is essential that a ladder of the correct length is used. It must extend at least 3ft 6ins above the highest rung from which the operator will be working. A ladder should be set at the correct angle for safe working with the base 1 foot out for every 4 feet up. For example if the ladder is resting at a height of 20 feet the ladder should be 5 feet away at the base.

Ladders must not be painted as this tends to mask defects in the timber or metal. In the case of wooden ladders preservation can be achieved by applying clear varnish or using a transparent rot-proofing liquid. Painting ladders is prohibited under the Construction (Working Places) Regulations 1966.

Ladders should be protected from continual exposure to weather and should be stored in a reasonably cool dry area. There should be free air circulation and adequate support to prevent the development of warping or weakening of the joints. Ladders should be supported only on the lower stiles. They should not be hung so that the weight is carried by the rungs but stored on edge clear of the ground on wall brackets. Ladders over 20 feet in length should have at least three points of support. All timber ladders should be stored well away from radiators, steam pipes or other sources of heat to avoid deformation. When carrying a ladder, single handed, special care should be taken when passing through doorways or around corners. The front end should be kept high enough to clear a person's head. Before turning care should be taken to ensure that both ends will clear all persons and objects in the vicinity.

Ladders should never be placed on boxes, bricks, barrels or other unstable bases. To obtain additional height a longer ladder should be used. Where extension ladders are used the minimum overlap of sections when the ladder is fully extended should be as follows:

Closed length feet	Minimum Overlap feet
up to 14	2ft
15 to 17	2ft 6in
18 to 20	3ft
21 to 23	3ft 6in
24 to 26	4ft

If a ladder has metal reinforcements on one side only it should be erected so that the reinforcement is on the under, or tension, side of the stiles. A ladder should always be used the right way round. Rung ties should be underneath the rungs. The extending stage should always be on top of the previous stage. The top of the ladder should be placed against a firm support on which both stiles will rest securely. A ladder should never be rested against a window sash. A board may be lashed across the top of the ladder to give a bearing on each side of the window.

A ladder should be secured to prevent slipping by lashing it firmly at the top. This will prevent it slipping sideways or the foot from slipping outwards. If lashing at the top is not possible a person should be stationed at the foot to hold it firmly. Alternatively the bottom of the ladder may be lashed to a convenient fixture to prevent it slipping outwards. When a ladder is erected at a place in which traffic is liable to be passing a man should be placed on guard or a space around the base of the ladder fenced off. Similarly if a ladder is to be erected in the vicinity of a door the door should either be locked shut or secured in an open position. In the latter case a person should be placed on guard.

A ladder should be faced when ascending or descending with the hands gripping the stiles or rungs. Nothing should be carried in the hands when ascending or descending a ladder. Tools or other small items should be carried in a belt or special shoulder bag but all large items or materials should be carried in a belt by means of a suitable line, rope or tackle from a safe position.

When working on a ladder it should be held with one hand unless a safety belt is used. It is important to ensure that the ladder is firmly secured before using a safety belt.

APPENDIX I

FIRST AID

Hints

Bleeding and wounds

For wounds with severe bleeding apply firm pressure on bleeding point at once and keep there until the dressing is ready. Apply dressing, a pad and bandage firmly. Send for the doctor. Small wounds with little bleeding apply dressing, a pad and bandage.

Bleeding from the Nose

Sit casualty by open window. Incline head forward and instruct him to breathe through the mouth. Gently pinch the front soft parts of the nose. Loosen tight clothing around the neck.

Burns and Scalds

If minor immerse affected part in cold running water. Cover with sterile dressing or clean laundered linen and bandage lightly. Do NOT apply lotions or ointments. If injury is severe take casualty to hospital. Do NOT break blisters.

Clothing on Fire

Wrap casualty quickly in a blanket, rug or coat. Lay him on the ground and beat out the flames. If alone do not rush out of doors if your clothing is alight. Wrap yourself in a coat or rug and roll on the floor. Call for help.

Drowning

Expired air method. The patient should be laid flat on his back and the clothing around his neck and chest loosened. Tilt the patient's head back ensuring that there is no blockage of the airway. Pinch the patient's nostrils together, seal your lips round his mouth and blow into the lungs until the chest rises. Remove your mouth breathe in and repeat rhythmically for four quick inflations before slowing to normal breathing rate.

Shock

This condition results from accidents or sudden illness and is characterised by faintness, pallor, coldness, feeling of sickness, vomiting and even unconsciousness. It is a serious condition. Treat by laying the casualty down on back, head low and reassure him. Always handle injured and sick people with great care as pain increases shock. If signs and symptoms do not quickly disappear then get casualty to hospital as soon as possible.

Stings

Remove the sting if it can be seen and apply surgical spirit or a solution of bicarbonate of soda. If the sting is in the throat wash out with a solution of bicarbonate of soda and water.

Unconsciousness

An unconscious casualty must have medical attention. Place him in the recovery position and do not attempt to give anything by the mouth. If a person feels faint get his head down. If sitting put the head between the knees and apply smelling salts with care. All cases should have plenty of fresh air. Loosen the clothing at neck, chest and waist.

Diagram of Recovery Position

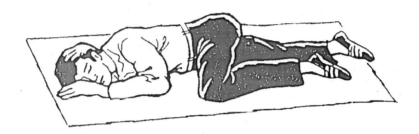

Artificial respiration

The Expired Air Method

This method of artificial respiration is considered more effective than the manual methods because, whilst it has the same advantage in that it can be carried out by a single operator, it produces better ventilation of the lungs than the manual methods. This is of the utmost importance as a lack of oxygen in the blood supply to the brain will cause irreparable damage to the nerve cells in a very short time – a matter of a few minutes. Whatever method is used it is essential that artificial respiration be given as quickly as possible.

How to carry out expired air resuscitation.

1. Lay the patient on his back and, if on a slope, have the stomach slightly lower than the chest.
2. Make a brief inspection of the mouth and throat to ensure that they are clear of any obvious obstruction.
3. Give the patient's head the maximum backward tilt so that the chin is prominent and the neck stretched to give a clear airway.
4. Open your mouth wide make an airtight seal over the mouth of the patient and blow. The operator's cheek or the hand supporting the chin can be used to seal the patient's nose.

89

5. Or if his mouth cannot be used close the patient's mouth using the hand supporting the chin open your mouth wide and make an airtight seal over his nose and blow.
   This may be used as an alternative to the mouth-to-mouth technique when the nose is not blocked. The wrist must be kept low on the patient's forehead to ensure that the full tilt of the head is maintained.
6. After exhaling turn your head to watch for chest movement whilst inhaling deeply in readiness for blowing again.
7. If the chest does not rise check that the patient's mouth and throat are free of obstruction and his head is tilted backwards as far as possible. Blow again.
8. If air enters the patient's stomach through blowing too hard press the stomach gently with the head of the patient turned to one side.
9. Commence resuscitation with 4 quick inflations of the patient's chest to give rapid build-up of oxygen in the patient's blood and then slow down to 16-18 respirations per minute or blow again each time the patient's chest has deflated. With small children and babies inflation at the rate of twenty a minute is achieved by a series of puffs each one ceasing as the chest starts to rise.
   UNDER NO CIRCUMSTANCES BLOW VIOLENTLY INTO A BABY'S LUNGS.
10. Whilst preparing to commence resuscitation breathe deeply with the mouth open to build up the oxygen content.

General rules for Treatment of Fractures

   a. Asphyxia, unconsciousness and severe bleeding must be dealt with first.
   b. Treat fracture where casualty lies unless:
      i. There is immediate danger to life of casualty in which case he must be moved quickly.
      ii. There is danger but time will allow the fracture to be temporarily secured and supported for movement to a safe place.
   c. Steady and support injured part at once. Maintain this control until fracture is completely secured.
   d. Immobilise fracture by securing injured part to sound part of body with bandages. These should be applied sufficiently tightly to prevent movement but NOT so tightly as to interfere with circulation or cause pain.
   e. Unless there is danger to casualty or First Aider, or weather is very bad, it is better NOT to move casualty until the ambulance arrives. This avoids moving the casualty unnecessarily.
   f. If the ambulance is expected to arrive within 10-15 minutes it is preferable to support the injured part in the most comfortable position by use of rolled up blankets or other materials.

To Treat a Fractured Arm – Elbow not Involved

    a. Place injured arm across casualty's chest and gently support.

    b. Apply adequate soft padding between limb and chest. If wrist or forearm injured place in fold of soft padding.

    c. Support arm in arm sling.

    d. Give further support by securing upper limb to chest by broad bandage applied over sling tied in front on uninjured side.

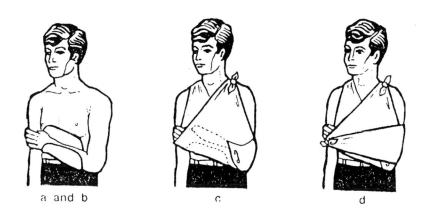

a and b   c.   d

To Treat a Fractured Arm-Elbow Cannot be Bent

    a. DO NOT attempt to force limb.

    b. Lay casualty down and place injured limb by his side.

    c. Apply adequate soft padding between injured limb and body.

    d. Secure injured arm to body by three broad bandages, one around upper arm and trunk, one around forearm and trunk, one around wrist an thighs; all tied on uninjured side of body.

    e. Prepare casualty for transport as stretcher case.

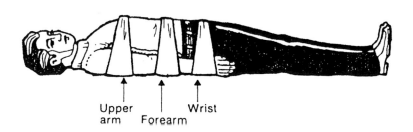

Upper   Wrist
arm   Forearm

91

To Treat a Fractured Lower Limb

Locations

    a. Neck of thigh bone.
    b. Thigh bone.
    c. Lower leg – one or both bones.

Symptons and Signs

    a. Neck of thigh bone – foot falls outwards, leg shortened.
    b. Thigh bone – shortening and swelling.
    c. Lower leg – usually open.

Treatment

    a. Lay casualty down.
    b. Carefully steady and support limb.
    c. Place bandages in position under feet and knees.
    d. Place adequate soft padding or padded splint between limbs.
    e. Bring uninjured limb alongside injured and support both limbs.
    f. Place additional padding to fill spaces between limbs.
    g. Tie bandages on uninjured side.
    h. Place soft padding under knots.

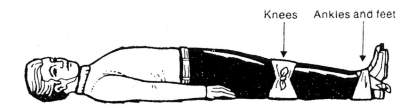

Knees   Ankles and feet

APPENDIX II

CONVERSION TABLES

The most commonly used metric units are:
length in METRES   (m)
weight in GRAMMES   (g)
capacity in LITRES   (l)

Prefixes are used with these basic units. The most common are:
kilo (k)   —   1000 times unit
deca (da)   —   10 times unit
milli (m)   —   1/1000 of unit
centi (c)   –   1/100 of unit
For example: 100 centimetres (cm)   =   1 metre (m)
                1000 metres   (m)   =   1 kilometre (km)

Some metric equivalents:
Length:
1 in   –   2.54 cm   1 mm   =   0.039 in
1 ft   =   30.48 cm   1 cm   =   0.394 in
1 yd   =   0.9144 m   1 m   =   1.094 yd
1 mile   =   1.609 km   1 km   =   0.621 mile

Area:
$1 in^2$ = $6.45 cm^2$ $1 cm^2$ = $0.155 in^2$
$1 ft^2$ = $929 cm^2$ $1 m^2$ = $1.196 yd^2$
$1 yd^2$ = $0.836 m^2$ $1 m^2$ = $10.764 ft^2$
$1 mile^2$ = $2.59 km^2$ $1 km^2$ = $0.386 mile^2$

Weight:
1 oz   =   28.35 g   1 g   =   0.0353 oz
1 lb   =   453.6 g   1 kg   =   2.2046 lb
1 cwt   =   50.802 kg   1 kg   =   0.0197 cwt
1 ton   =   1016.04 kg   1 tonne   =   0.984 tons
   (2240 lb)   (1000 kg)

93

Volume:

$1\,in^3$	=	$16.39cm^3$	$1cm^3$	=	$0.061in^3$
$1\,ft^3$	=	$28,317cm^3$	$1m^3$	=	$35.32ft^3$
$1\,yd^3$	=	$0.765m^3$	$1m^3$	=	$1.31yd^3$

Capacity:

1 fl.oz.	=	28.4ml	1 ml	=	0.0352 fl.oz.
1 pint	=	568ml	1 l	=	1.76 pints
1 Imp. gal.	=	4.546 l	1 l	=	0.22 Imp Gals.
			1 l	=	35.2 fl.oz.

Useful factors:

1 teaspoonful	=	⅛ fl.oz
1 tablespoonful	=	½ fl.oz.
1 Imp. pint	=	20 fl.oz.
¼ Imp. gal	=	40 fl.oz

1 gal. water (at 62°F) weighs 10 lb
1 litre water (at 62°F) weighs 2.2 lb

Thermometrical:

Fahrenheit:	freezing point	=	32°
	boiling point	=	212°
Celcius:	freezing point	=	0°
	boiling point	=	100°

To convert Fahrenheit to Celcius:
$$(°F-32) \times \frac{5}{9} = °C$$
e.g. to convert 68°F to Celcius; $(68-32) \times \frac{5}{9} = 36 \times \frac{5}{9} = 20°C$

To convert Celcius to Fahrenheit:
$$(°C \times \frac{9}{5}) + 32 = °F$$
e.g. to convert 20°C to Farenheit; $(20 \times \frac{9}{5}) + 32 = 36 + 32 = 68°F$

APPENDIX III

COMMERCIAL PHRASES AND ABBREVIATIONS

ad hoc (Latin) For that particular purpose.
ad infinitum (Latin) Without end.
ad libitum (ad lib) (Latin) At pleasure, to any extent.
Ad nauseam (Latin) Until disgusted. To a sickening degree.
ad valorem (ad val) (Latin) In proportion to value.
à la carte (French) Item by item from a bill of fare.
Alias (Latin) Otherwise.
Alibi (Latin) Elsewhere.
Appraise. To value goods or property.
a priori (Latin) From the cause to the effect.
au fait (French) Well acquainted with.
Bona fide (Latin) In good faith.
carte blanche (French) Without restriction.
c.f. (**confer**) Compare.
circa (**c**) (Latin) About (time).
Consignee. The party to whom goods are consigned.
Consignor. The party who consigns, or sends, goods to another.
contra (Latin) Against.
Creditor. One to whom money is owing.
Dei gratia (Latin) By the Grace of God.
de jure (Latin) By right.
D.V. (**Deo volente**) God willing.
e.g. exempli gratia (Latin) For example.
E. and O.E. Errors and omissions excepted.
etc. et ceteri or cetera (Latin) And others, and so forth.
et sequentia (**et seq**) (Latin) And the following.
ex gratia (Latin) As an act of grace or goodwill.
ex officia (Latin) By virtue of office.
ex parte (Latin) On one side only.
f.o.b. Free on board **f.o.c.** Free of charge.
force majeure (French) Circumstances beyond one's control.
Guarantor. One who makes a guarantee.
Guaranty. A warrant of surety; a contract to see performed what another has undertaken
Ibidem (**ibid**) (Latin) In the same place.

95

idem (id) (Latin) The same.

id est (i.e.) (Latin) That is.

Indemnity. Security from damage or loss, compensation for loss or injury.

infra dig. infra dignititatem (Latin) Beneath one's dignity; undignified.

Inst. Instant. Present month.

Inter alia (Latin) Among other things.

Invoice. A letter of advice of the despatch of goods, with particulars of their price and quantity.

I.O.U. A memorandum of debt given by a borrower to a lender, requiring no stamp, but to be wholly written by the borrower, dated and addressed to some person.

ipso facto (Latin) By the fact itself.

Lessee. Holder of, tenant (of house, etc.) under lease.

Lessor. Person who lets on lease.

Letter of Credit. A letter empowering the bearer to obtain money from the party addressed.

locum tenens (Latin) A temporary substitute.

modus operandi (Latin) Plan of working.

Moratorium. A legal authorisation to a debtor to postpone payment for a certain time.

Mortgage. A charge of real property as security for money lent.

Mortgagee. One to whom a mortgage is made or given. The person who lends the money.

Mortgagor. The person who mortgages or charges his property as security for debt. The borrower.

nem. con. (Nemine contradicente) (Latin) Without opposition; no one contradicting.

Nominee. One who is nominated by another.

non sequitur (Latin) It does not follow.

nota bene (n.b.) (Latin) Note well.

onus (Latin) Burden.

par. Equality of nominal and market value.

pari passu (Latin) On an equal footing.

Payee. One to whom money is paid.

per (Latin) Through; by means of; according to.

per cent, % (Latin) per centum, by the hundred.

per procurationem (p.p. or pro) Signed by an authorised person on behalf of his principal.

per se (Latin) By itself; considered apart.

Post date. To date a document in advance of the real date.

Post restante. Post Office department where postal packets remain until called for.

P.S. Post scriptum (Latin) Post script.

Power of attorney. A document which empowers one person to act for another.

prima facie (Latin) At the first glance.

pro bono publico (Latin) For the public good.

Promissory note. A signed note containing a promise to pay a sum of money to a named person, or to bearer, on a specified date, or at sight, or on demand. Note-Stamp duty is required.

pro rata (Latin) Proportionately

Pro tempore (Pro tem.) (Latin) For the time being.

prox. Proximo. Next month.

Proxy. A deputy; a stamped power of attorney or authority to vote or act for another.

q.e. (quod est) (Latin) Which is.

q.e.d. (quod erat demonstradum) (Latin) Which was to be demonstrated or proved.

quid pro quo (Latin) One thing for another.

q.v. (quid vide) (Latin) Which see.

Rate of Exchange. The value of one currency in terms of another.

Rebate. An allowance made as discount.

R.I.P. (requiescat in pace) (Latin) Rest in peace.

R.S.V.P. (respondez, s'il vous plait) (French) Please reply.

sic (Latin) Thus, so given.

sine die (Latin) Indefinitely; without a day.

sin qua non (Latin) An indispensable condition.

status quo (Latin) Existing state of affairs.

stet (Latin) Let it stand (Printing).

subpoena (Latin) A writ commanding the attendance of a person in court under a penalty.

table d'hote (French) Dinner, etc., served in hotel or restaurant at a fixed hour and price; opposite to à la carte.

ult., ultimo (Latin) In preceding month.

ultra vires (Latin) Beyond their powers.

v., versus (Latin) Against.

vice versa (Latin) The order being changed.

vide (Latin) See.

vis a vis (French) Opposite; face to face.

Without prejudice. Leaving the question open.

INDEX

98